OTHER GCD BOOKS

Visit GCDiscipleship.com/books

The Sermon on the Mount: A 31 Day Guide Through Jesus' Teaching by Tracy Richardson

Sent Together: How the Gospel Sends Leaders to Start Missional Communities by Brad Watson

The Stories We Live: Discovering the True and Better Way of Jesus by Sean Post

Make, Mature, Multiply: Becoming Fully-Formed Disciples of Jesus edited by Brandon D. Smith

Called Together: A Guide to Forming Missional Communities by Jonathan K. Dodson and Brad Watson

everPresent: How the Gospel Relocates Us in the Present by Jeremy Writebol

SMALL TOWN MISSION

a guide for mission-driven communities

SMALL TOWN MISSION

a guide for mission-driven communities

AARON MORROW

GCD BOOKS

ISBN-13: 978-0692712825
ISBN-10: 0692712828

Cover design by Andy Burchardt
andyburchardt.com

Cover drawing by Justin Hilden
justinhilden.com

Dedicated to my friends Jeff Nettles, Ethan Johnson, Jeff Suits, Matt Wunderlin, Paul Glendenning, Mike Majeski, and Jason Sasse.

All of them are current or former pastors in Platteville, which is a small town in southwest Wisconsin. They've modeled for me what it means to prioritize the local church and be on mission in a small town for the sake of the gospel.

They are the best at what they do.

CONTENTS

INTRODUCTION

I grew up on a farm.

Tractors, cattle, crops, big machinery, freezing cold winters, too many cats, and a marathon bus ride to school every morning. That's right, I grew up on a farm. And that farm was next to a small town that my family and I called home. I've lived in small towns for most of my life, even after I moved away from the herd of cats. The small towns I've lived in may not be as cool as Austin or have the trendy conveniences of Seattle, but small towns will always be a part of who I am. If you live in a small town, you might know what I mean.

According to the US census, just over half of our population lives in towns, boroughs, villages, and townships with fewer than 25,000 people or in rural areas. Meanwhile, thousands of Christian books are published every year and hundreds of these are about mission and reaching people for Christ. Many of them have insightful and helpful ideas about mission that can be applied anywhere, but many of their ideas don't seem to work in small towns. We should be thankful for resources like these, but we also need resources written specifically for mission in small towns.

A friend at my church has said that books about reaching people in closed countries in the 10/40 window relate best to mission in small towns because residents often have hardened religious mindsets and impenetrable circuits of relationships. My friend is probably exaggerating the comparison, but I understand what he's saying because mission in small towns can be incredibly difficult and complicated.

KEEPING THE END IN MIND

Being on mission isn't my primary aim in writing this book. Even though this book is about mission, mission is not the ultimate goal of our lives. Pastor John Piper writes,

> Missions is not the ultimate goal of the church. Worship is. Missions exists because worship doesn't. Worship is ultimate, not missions, because God is ultimate, not man. When this age is over, and the countless millions of the redeemed fall on their faces before the throne of God, missions will be no more. It is a temporary necessity. But worship abides forever.[1]

We are designed to be worshippers of Jesus who find our identity in him. Imagine if you found your identity in being on mission and successfully winning people to Christ. If that's you, eternity will jolt you because there are no unbelievers in heaven. Let's keep the perspective that being on mission is a temporary necessity. From now through eternity, Jesus should be the focus and goal of everything we do, including being on mission to reach people with the gospel. While mission isn't the ultimate goal of our lives, worshippers of Jesus are on mission because it's the indisputable by-product of worshiping him. My hope and prayer is that you worship your way through this book and, as a result, many people in your town will turn to Jesus and worship him with you.

---

1 John Piper. *Let the Nations Be Glad: The Supremacy of God in Missions*, 2nd ed. Grand Rapids, MI: Baker Academic, 2003. 17.

REGULAR FOLK

Small towns are in desperate need of missionaries. When I say missionaries, I'm not referring to the pastor of your church or people who suffer for Jesus by building huts and preaching to native islanders. No, I'm referring to regular people. Small towns desperately need normal, everyday people like farmers, factory workers, teachers, secretaries, and small business owners who think and act like missionaries to reach their friends, neighbors, co-workers, and extended families for Christ. Pastors in small towns should be deeply respected for their incredible hearts to advance the gospel. However, the responsibility of mission is given to all believers, not just pastors. If you are a Christian, you are sent to be on mission regardless of where you live or what your job is.

BUILDING FENCE

Almost every resource about mission is based on a certain way of doing ministry and, in some ways, this book is no different (more about that later). Some resources seem to take a self-righteous tone by telling us and our church how to do ministry in our town. That's not my goal. We've all read books or articles like that and found them a bit off-putting. My goal is to help you better understand principles of mission in small towns instead of offering a rigid prescription for you and your church. In the matter of mission in your town, remember to follow the lead of your church's leaders because Scripture is clear that they are the ones you must submit to (Hebrews 13:17). My hope is to come alongside your church, not to replace the authority of your church's leaders.

One of my least favorite jobs on the farm was building fence. My dad always said he felt great satisfaction after making a well-built fence. I have no idea what he was talking about. If you've never built a wire fence, it's actually much harder than it seems. But I did manage to learn that an important part of successfully building a wire fence is to have a series of anchor posts that will support the rolls of wire. Similarly, our study of mission in small towns requires a few unique anchor posts to support it. They aren't the only anchor posts that should be present in a church, but the ones listed below should help you better understand and engage the ideas in this book.

Anchor Post #1: Gospel-Centered

The gospel is the good news of God's grace invading the darkness of this world. It is the grand narrative of creation, fall, redemption, and consummation ordained by God and orchestrated through the life, death, resurrection, and ascension of Jesus Christ. Christ's crucifixion is the heart of the gospel. His resurrection is the power of the gospel. His ascension is the glory of the gospel.[2]

But what does it mean to be gospel-centered? When people talk about it, they're often saying it in one of two ways. First, people use it as a lens to view all of our spiritual growth as dependent on the gospel. At the end of the day, all spiritual growth happens in the midst of our ongoing struggle with sin and our ongoing need for grace through Christ to invade the darkness of our hearts. Dane Ortland says,

> This is why Paul constantly reminds people—reminds Christian people—of the Gospel (Romans 1:16–17; 1 Corinthians 1:18; 15:3–4; Galatians 1:6). We move forward in discipleship not mainly through pep talks and stern warnings. We move forward when we hear afresh the strangeness of grace, relaxing our hearts and loosening our clenched hold on a litany of lesser things—financial security, the perfect spouse, career

---

2 The Village Church. Statement of Faith. www.thevillagechurch.net. Accessed February 11, 2016.

advancement, sexual pleasure, human approval, and so on.[3]

Second, people use it to refer to how the gospel shapes our outlook on everything in life and ministry. This would include how we understand politics, social action, ethics in the workplace and elsewhere in the public sphere, being on mission in a small town, and countless other related examples. In this sense, the gospel is actively forming how we look at and understand everything in our lives and the world around us.

Being on mission to reach non-Christians is obviously important because hell is hot and forever is a long time. But more importantly, we must be on mission in a gospel-centered way if we want mission to be healthy and sustainable. Growing in a gospel-centered way gives our mission authenticity and frees us from the burden of "do better and try harder." Mission in light of the gospel is intrinsically found in God's nature; knowing this helps us see mission as something to be naturally integrated into our lives as followers of Christ, as opposed to just another thing to add to our already busy schedule.

Anchor Post #2: The Local Church

If we aren't committed to a local church, that's a big problem. It's impossible to reconcile mission apart from the local church because the New Testament constantly emphasizes mission in the context of the local church, not makeshift spiritual gatherings. If we want to be aligned with the New Testament, we can't be on mission to our friends, neighbors, and co-workers without also aiming to prioritize the flourishing of our local church. And even though some local churches are more challenging than others to be invested in,

---

3 Dane Ortland. The Gospel Coalition. http://www.thegospelcoalition.org/article/whats-all-this-gospel-cent ered-talk-about. Accessed September 16, 2014.

the Holy Spirit can empower us to be patient and loving to any group of people, just as he is with us! In the end, the gospel needs to form how we think and feel about the local church.

Furthermore, this book embraces a missionary understanding of the local church. This doesn't mean that mission is the only thing that a church does, but it does mean that mission must be prioritized. That's because mission is an essential element of a local church's identity as an outworking of the gospel.

Anchor Post #3: Equipping People

Churches that are committed to seeing their people as missionaries should also be committed to equipping their people for being on mission. Equipping means discipling and training people to think and act like missionaries and sending them on mission in their spheres of influence (i.e., where they live, where they work, where they play, what their kids are involved in, etc). In Ephesians 4:11–12, the Apostle Paul says,

> It was he who gave some to be apostles, some to be prophets, some to be evangelists, and some to be pastors and teachers, to prepare God's people for works of service, so that the body of Christ may be built up.

Pastor J. D. Greear has said that, in light of Ephesians 4:11–12, the day he became a pastor was the day he left the ministry because God gave pastors to the church to equip people for the work of ministry.[4] Greear is obviously overstating his point for effect, but I generally agree with what's he's saying.

The discipling and training process for sending people on mission is crucial for a church that wants to be on mission. It's also worth noting that most churches who are

---

4 J. D. Greear. The Exchange with Ed Stetzer. https://vimeo.com/140949635.

committed to this process aren't overly committed to getting non-Christians to attend the church's programs and facilities. Granted, getting non-Christians to attend a church's programs and facilities can be good and helpful, especially in small towns that are filled with non-Christians who have a more traditional mindset about how churches function. However, if this strategy isn't accompanied by a primary strategy of discipling, training, and sending, the church will probably and eventually be filled with people who expect pastors and programs to do the work of mission for them.

Anchor Post #4: Mission in Community

Ministry is meant to happen in the context of relationships because all of us, whether we realize it or not, have a deep need and desire to know and be known by others. We have been made in the image of God, who has eternally existed in community as the Father, Son, and Holy Spirit. We are designed to be in relationship and community with others. This is why we should do mission in the context of relationships and biblical community as much as possible.

This book wasn't written for lone rangers to read it by themselves. Instead, it was written for two or more people to go through together, because making disciples who are on mission together is (or should be!) one of the priorities of the local church. That's why you should go through this with someone whom you want to be on mission with. This might include Christian neighbors, co-workers, members of your small group, or anyone you meet regularly with for discipleship. If you're married you might consider going through it with your spouse, because married couples who follow Jesus are on a permanent mission trip together. Even if you've been married for thirty years or more, don't underestimate what the Holy Spirit can do when it comes to aligning both your hearts and minds for the sake of mission.

I pray this book encourages you in your mission with Jesus so that more people can know and worship Jesus in your small town. After all, mission isn't just something that must be prioritized globally and in big cities; it must also be prioritized locally and in small towns.

HOW TO USE THIS BOOK

Each chapter is divided into two parts: Before You Meet and When You Meet.

Before You Meet

The first part is meant to be completed on your own, before you meet with the rest of your group. This part will always have a few questions for you to answer before you meet together.

When You Meet

The second part is meant to be completed when you meet together with your group. This part will encourage you to discuss the questions in the chapter, how your mindset has changed after reading the chapter, and how to pray together in response to the chapter.

Lastly, there are four simple ideas for mission at the end of each chapter that you should read together as a group. These ideas are meant to help you implement the content of the chapters in practical ways in the everyday spheres of your life: where you live, where you work, where you play, and what your kids are involved in (if you have kids).

It's not practical or realistic to implement every idea, so don't feel guilty for not being able to do it all. Even more importantly, we must remember that mission is something that should always stem from our identity in Christ. If it doesn't, then these ideas for mission will probably and eventually feel burdensome and crushing. The gospel of belonging to Christ through faith in him is what gives our life value and worth, which is something that zeal for mission can never do. Start with the gospel, let it give you identity, and let it lead you to mission!

PART 1

THE MISSION: THINKING LIKE A MISSIONARY

CHAPTER 1
BEING SENT

 **BEFORE YOU MEET**

"God, I'm really frustrated."

Kevin silently prayed this as he headed to the door for his nightly walk. He had finally finished the dishes, the kids were in bed, and his wife was unwinding from a long day by reading a mystery novel. He exited past the refrigerator, which was filled with pictures of overseas missionaries that their family prayed for on a regular basis.

Walking around the neighborhood in their small town was Kevin's way to relax after being cooped up in the office all day. But this was also his time to talk to God, because most of his days were filled with busyness and interruptions. Kevin walked past several houses in his neighborhood, many of which had their lights on.

"I love all those missionaries on the fridge who are doing crazy things for you all over the world," he prayed as he walked down the street, "but here it just seems like we're going through the motions of everyday life, and I guess I'm just frustrated by that." Kevin continued walking down the street while reflecting, "I'd love to hop on a plane and be a *missionary like them."*

Kevin could benefit from studying what Scripture says about being sent. Being sent is one of the mega-themes in the Gospel of John. Jesus identifies himself as being sent by the Father ten times in Matthew, Mark, and Luke, but Jesus identifies as being sent forty-two times in John. Look up all forty-two references in the Gospel of John (see chart below) but don't take notes, because we're trying to look at the forest, not the trees.

Jesus identifies himself as being sent from the Father in the Gospel of John:

3:17	*3:34*	*4:34*	*5:22–23*
5:24	*5:30*	*5:36–38 (3x)*	*6:29*
6:38–39 (2x)	*6:44*	*6:57*	*7:16*
7:18	*7:28–29 (2x)*	*7:33*	*8:16*
8:18	*8:26*	*8:29*	*8:42*
9:4	*10:36*	*11:42*	*12:44-45 (2x)*
12:49	*13:16*	*13:20*	*14:24*
15:21	*16:5*	*17:3*	*17:8*
17:18	*17:20-21*	*17:23*	*17:25*

When someone is sent to a specific place with a specific mission, that person is a missionary. In the case of Jesus, he was sent to earth where he traded the comforts of the heavenly culture for the discomforts of the earthly culture. This was a big deal because he was born in a barn, swung a hammer with his dad, mourned the death of his cousin, sweated blood, and was brutally murdered by his critics. His life was filled with discomfort and inconvenience. But he also came with a specific mission to preach the gospel, die for our sins, and rise from the dead so that he could forever intercede for us. Do you see the point? Jesus is God as a missionary.

The final instance of Jesus identifying himself as a missionary who is sent by the Father is the one that has the most application for us today.

> *On the evening of that first day of the week, when the disciples were together, with the doors locked for fear of the Jews, Jesus came and stood among them and said, "Peace be with you!" After he said this, he showed them his hands and side. The disciples were overjoyed when they saw the Lord. Again Jesus said, "Peace be with you! As the Father has sent me, I am sending you."*
> *– John 20:19–21*

Q1: Verse 20:21 is the key of this passage. Jesus says, "As the Father has sent me, I am sending you." How do you think this verse connects with the rest of the "sent" verses in John, and what implications does this have for how you view your life and ministry as a Christian?

Do you want to be like Jesus? If so, you need to wrestle with the fact that Jesus was a missionary. It is a life changing experience to realize that you worship a missionary. And that missionary is sending you on mission with him (Matthew 28:18–20), which is kind of like going to work with your dad. Going to work with your dad is awesome because you get the satisfaction of being with him, he will keep you from screwing up his work, and he's just glad you're there with him. This is the essence of what it means to be sent on mission with Jesus.

However, someone might rightfully point out that there is more to our discipleship than just being on mission. I agree. But our discipleship is never *less* than being on mission, either. That's why mission is always vital and essential for being a healthy and growing disciple of Jesus.

TO THE ENDS OF THE EARTH

Unfortunately, most Christians find it easier to think about being a missionary across the ocean than being a missionary across the street. In *Gospel-Centered Church*, Steve Timmis and Tim Chester[5] ask their readers to imagine themselves being part of a church planting team in a distant country. If you were in that situation, how would you answer the following questions? Write your answers below.

- What criteria would you use to decide where to live?

- How would you approach secular employment?

- What standard of living would you expect as pioneer missionaries?

- What would you spend your time doing?

---

5 Steve Timmis and Tim Chester. *Gospel-Centered Church: Becoming the Community God Wants You to Be*. Purcellville, VA: The Good Book Company, 2012. 12.

- What opportunities would you be looking for?

- What would you be praying about?

- What would you try to do with your new friends?

- What kind of team would you want around you?

Q2: Which of these questions stood out to you the most when you were answering them? Why did they stand out to you?

Q3: How do your answers to these questions compare with your life right now? Why do you think this is?

 # WHEN YOU MEET

The truth is that you're sent to be on mission in your small town just like if you were part of that church-planting team in a distant country. That's because God wants missionaries at the ends of the earth, at the end of the cul-de-sac, at the end of the cornfield, and at the end of the hallway at work. If you're a Christian then you have been sent, no matter where you are, because mission is a central purpose for us wherever we are.

- Discuss the three questions in this chapter.

- In what way has your mindset changed after reading this chapter?

- In response to this chapter and your discussion, what is the Holy Spirit leading you to pray about together?

Simple Ideas for Mission

Below are four simple ideas for mission, based on the average person's spheres of influence: where you live, where you work, where you play, and what your kids are involved in (if you don't have kids, feel free to ignore this one).

Again, it's not practical or realistic to implement every idea below, so don't feel guilty for not being able to do it all.

But even more importantly, we must remember that mission is something that should always stem from our identity in Christ. If it doesn't, then these ideas for mission will eventually feel burdensome and crushing. The gospel of belonging to Christ through faith in him is what gives our life value and worth, which is something that zeal for mission can never do. Start with the gospel, let it give you identity, and let it lead you to mission!

As a group, please read the simple ideas for mission below.

 ## WHERE YOU LIVE

Consider inviting your neighbors who aren't Christians over for supper. An easy way to not let this slip your mind is to make a list of neighbors who you want to prioritize over the next six months to invite over. God has put you in your neighborhood on purpose, so prayerfully consider how he might administer his love and grace through your hospitality.

 ## WHERE YOU WORK

If your schedule allows for it, consider being intentional about regularly spending time with co-workers for a few minutes after work instead of quickly rushing home when it's quitting time. If you do this on a regular basis, consider the cumulative effect this would have over the course of several years in terms of building relationships and trust. Pray regularly about these conversations.

WHERE YOU PLAY

Consider hosting a party to watch your favorite sporting event. This is an easy idea for the sake of mission since you're probably going to be watching the game anyway. Invite both your Christian and non-Christian friends and neighbors so that your friendship networks can start overlapping in a purposeful way.

🐻 YOUR KIDS

If you have kids, consider volunteering to coach your kids' sports teams this summer. Introduce yourself to all the other parents, host a team party at your house where parents are invited along with their kids, and make being on the team a fun experience for everyone. Coaching little kids can often be challenging, but it's an easy way to connect with people for the sake of mission.

CHAPTER 2
FOUR TRAPS THAT KILL MISSION

 **BEFORE YOU MEET**

"So what do you think about it?"

It was small group night, and Bill and Melinda were leading the group. Bill was trying to lead a conversation about non-Christians and our attitudes about mission. And then the conversation started to go sideways.

"We need to be careful we aren't falling into the snare of sin when we're around non-Christians because, first and foremost, we're called as Christians to be holy," stated one concerned member of the group.

"I don't know," another member countered, "I don't think we should be uptight about managing our sin. After all, if we're going to reach non-Christians then we need to actually relate to them."

"I couldn't agree more that this nation needs to turn to God so that our land will be healed," another member awkwardly asserted. "My prayer is that God will raise up a

generation of leaders in our capital that will hedge us in the right direction."

"You know, in troubling times like these, we need to realize that God is in control when it comes to moving the gospel forward," noted another member, "so the best thing for us to do is follow Jesus, keep reading our Bibles, and focus on our families."

Bill wasn't sure what to say next.

The people in Bill and Melinda's small group are actually struggling with the same things that people have struggled with for centuries, including people who interacted with Jesus during his time on earth. During his earthly ministry, four primary religious sects existed within Jewish culture: Pharisees, Sadducees, Zealots, and Essenes. Each of them had a particular view of how to interact with people outside of their group. Two thousand years later, their views are still instructive for us as we examine various traps that kill the effectiveness of the mission Jesus sent us on.[6]

Trap #1: Separating from Non-Christians like a Pharisee

The Pharisees were a very conservative group that was extremely committed to being holy and uncorrupted by the world. They were also very critical and judgmental towards non-Christians[7] because they didn't think non-Christians were as committed to following God as they were. And they were convinced that one of the easiest ways to be polluted by the

---

6 The original idea for these "traps" comes from the cultural "ruts" in the book *The Radical Reformission: Reaching Out without Selling Out* by Mark Driscoll.

7 Some readers will notice that I am using the word non-Christian when referring to people outside of each religious group. This isn't technically correct since people weren't called Christians until Antioch in Acts 11:26. But I'm choosing to use the word non-Christian so we can more clearly see the application.

world was to be around non-Christians. The last thing the Pharisees wanted to do was be influenced by non-Christians, so they avoided them like the plague in an effort to be holy.

We fall into this trap today when we stay away from non-Christians in an effort to be holy and when we organize our lives in such a way that we rarely have to spend time with them unless we're forced to, like family gatherings or going to work. This kind of thinking is flawed because that's not how we become holy, and it lacks the heart of God for people who are far from him. Let's briefly examine what the Bible says about this.

> *"My prayer is not that you take them out of the world but that you protect them from the evil one. They are not of the world, even as I am not of it. Sanctify them by the truth; your word is truth. As you sent me into the world, I have sent them into the world."*
> *– John 17:15–18*

In John 17:15, Jesus prays that we wouldn't be taken out of the world but that we would be protected from the evil of Satan. In other words, Jesus is praying against spiritual warfare and the allure of hunkering down and separating ourselves from non-Christians. Unfortunately, many Christians throughout history have separated themselves from non-Christians in an effort to become more holy. But do we actually become holy when we do this? Jesus would probably say we are missing the point, because he says that the truth in the word of God is what makes us holy (v. 17). In other words, the way we become holy isn't by avoiding non-Christians but by staying in a close relationship to Jesus because the entire word of God points to him (John 5:37–40). Staying connected to Jesus transforms our heart to mirror his heart for others, and we actively pursue relationships with non-Christians in hopes of loving them and connecting them with him. This actually protects us from sin, because the most healthy and sustainable way to avoid sin isn't to avoid non-Christians but to stick close to Jesus. Sticking close to him transforms everything about us and one of the natural expressions of sticking close to him is to be on mission (v. 18).

However, non-Christians aren't typically going to encourage us to stick close to Jesus, so how can we be faithful to John 17:15–18? When the average Christian thinks about mission, they typically think about doing it as a lone ranger. This is a horrible mindset because Christians who do mission alone often become frustrated, discouraged, and can easily fall prey to their own sinful desires. That's why we should always be on mission with at least one other Christian for the purpose of encouragement and accountability. This can be a spouse, friend, neighbor, co-worker, or classmate. Are you alone on mission? If so, you should start praying that God would bring Christians to your work, school, or neighborhood to be on mission with you, because God is in the business of sending out missionaries who aren't lone rangers (Luke 10:1–2).

Q1: In your own words, how does this trap kill mission, and in what ways do you fall into this trap?

Trap #2: Blending in with Non-Christians like a Sadducee

The Sadducees wanted badly to be accepted by non-Christians. They successfully avoided the trap of shunning non-Christians like the Pharisees did but they also failed to avoid the trap of blending in with them in a sinful way. They even went so far as to deny the existence of angels and demons as well as any kind of future resurrection for worshippers of God (Mark 12:18–27; Acts 23:8). In the end, their mission to reach out and influence non-Christians was undermined by their mission to be loved and accepted.

We fall into this trap today when being loved and accepted by non-Christians becomes more important to us than Jesus and his mission. Granted, there's nothing inherently wrong with being loved and accepted by non-Christians, but our mission of advancing the gospel will always be stuck in neutral if we also have a competing mission of being loved and accepted by them. In Luke 16:13, Jesus says, "No servant can serve two masters. Either he will hate the one and love the other, or he will be devoted to the one and despise the other. You cannot serve both God and money." Jesus is talking about money, but the same principle can be applied to mission because we can never serve two masters or missions that are competing for our allegiance. Jesus is our master and his mission deserves our full allegiance.

Q2: In your own words, how does this trap kill mission, and in what ways do you fall into this trap?

Trap #3: Ruling over Non-Christians like a Zealot

The Zealots misunderstood the difference between the kingdom of God and their own personal kingdom and, as a result, sought to usher it in through power and authority. This explains why they loved politics so much. The Zealots thought political systems were powerful tools in forcing non-Christians to be moral and obey the Bible. While in some ways this was well-intentioned, their fascination with power and politics only served to undermine their mission to influence non-Christians, because the gospel's way of transforming a non-Christian's morality is centered on giving them a new heart. When we become Christians, God puts a new heart in us (Jeremiah 24:7, 31:31–33, 32:39–40; Ezekiel 11:19–20, 36:26–27). With this new heart comes new thoughts, emotions, and desires that we didn't have before we were Christians. And it's out of the overflow of this new heart that we are changed from the inside out. In other words, deep changes in our heart don't ultimately come through gaining the political upper hand.

We fall into this trap today when we get more excited about candidates than the cross, when we are more interested in sermons about politics than in sermons about Jesus, and when we believe that if we simply elect more people who think like us then our country will be a terrific place. However, we must also realize that political systems need people who love Jesus, because policies and laws affect all of us. But even so, we also must realize that we don't need fair and just political systems in order to accomplish the mission Jesus gave us in John 20:21. If that were true, why has the church been exploding with conversions over the last fifty years in nations that are wildly corrupt and ungodly? Even though fair and just political systems are good for everyone, the hope of our mission is found in Jesus and not politics.

Q3: In your own words, how does this trap kill mission, and in what ways do you fall into this trap?

Trap #4: Ignoring Non-Christians like an Essene

The Essenes were an intense religious group that happily kept to themselves. They lived together in what we would consider a hippy commune where they would withdraw from non-Christians and ignore them. They did this so that they could focus their time and energy on their spiritual growth and encounter with God—as an isolated community. This isolation also had political motivation, but it hindered their mission because they weren't interested in the pursuit of God for those outside of their community.

We fall into this trap today when we are so preoccupied with our own spiritual growth that we forget there are actually non-Christians in our small town that need Jesus just as much as we do. This mindset is often accidentally reinforced when *growing spiritually* is not clearly connected with mission. This is a big problem because if growing spiritually doesn't eventually result in being sent on mission then something is enormously lacking in our spiritual growth! And it's crazy how it doesn't take long for a new Christian to learn how to make ignoring non-Christians sound spiritual and mature. For example, how often have you heard these kinds of phrases below?

- *This season of my life really needs to be focused on me and Jesus.*
- *Evangelism is a good thing but what I really need to focus on is going deeper with God.*
- *My husband and I need to build ourselves up spiritually before we start thinking about mission.*

At the very least, there is a half-truth in these statements, because all of us should eagerly desire to grow in our walk with Christ. But in my experience, the people who say these types of phrases aren't using spiritual growth as a springboard to anything except more spiritual growth. The half-truth is that we need to be growing spiritually, but ignoring non-Christians is not the fruit of someone who is growing spiritually.

Q4: In your own words, how does this trap kill mission, and in what ways do you fall into this trap?

 # WHEN YOU MEET

- Discuss the four questions in this chapter.

- In what way has your mindset changed after reading this chapter?

- In response to this chapter and your discussion, what is the Holy Spirit leading you to pray about together?

Simple Ideas for Mission

Below are four simple ideas for mission based on the average person's spheres of influence: where you live, where you work, where you play, and what your kids are involved in (if you don't have kids, feel free to ignore this one).

It's not practical or realistic to implement every idea below, so don't feel guilty for not being able to do it all. But even more importantly, we must remember that mission is something that should always stem from our identity in Christ. If it doesn't, then these ideas for mission will eventually feel burdensome and crushing. The gospel of belonging to Christ through faith in him is what gives our life value and worth, which is something that zeal for mission can never do. Start with the gospel, let it give you identity, and let it lead you to mission!

As a group, please read the simple ideas for mission below.

WHERE YOU LIVE

Rule #1 for evangelism in your neighborhood: reputations are gained quickly and die slowly. What kind of reputation are you building? However, it's easy to accidentally idolize our reputation to the point that we don't ever take meaningful risks for the advancement of the gospel. Pray that God will give you clarity on how to manage the tension between building a reputation among your neighbors that points to the gospel and taking meaningful risks for the mission.

WHERE YOU WORK

Pray that you won't be self-righteous about the language of your co-workers. And if you really want to confront your co-workers about their language, please know that those situations almost never go well; you'll probably get labeled as someone who is eager to look down on others and, as a result, they'll probably never listen to what you say about the gospel. If you work in a professional environment, let your supervisor determine the standards of professionalism at your workplace. And if you are a supervisor, make sure to enforce standards of professionalism so that your company will be more successful and not because you're trying to force morality down the throats of those you supervise. Pray for the strength to genuinely love your co-workers in whatever spiritual state they're currently in and to resist the urge to clean the outside of the cup without first letting God clean the inside of it (Matthew 23:25–26).

⦿ WHERE YOU PLAY

If you want to have an effective witness for the gospel in your town, then you can't have a strong opinion about everything. If the non-Christians in your life see you as opinionated and critical when they see you around town, they'll probably have a hard time listening to your opinions about the gospel. And if you're always busy sharing your opinions at the coffee shop then it's probably going to be hard to find space in the conversation to talk about weightier matters of eternal importance.

🧸 YOUR KIDS

Don't just go to your kids' sporting events, go with a focus on mission and pray that you'll sit next to the other parents that God wants you to, instead of just sitting next to the parents that you know from church, who you're comfortable with. Pray that God will enable you to build relationships with non-Christian parents in these settings for the advancement of the mission.

PART 2
THE MISSION AND DEPENDENCE: RELYING ON GOD LIKE A MISSIONARY

CHAPTER 3
THE HOLY SPIRIT AND MISSION

 **BEFORE YOU MEET**

"I sharpened the blades on it for you."

Leroy unhooked the hay cutter and wound up the jack. It was the end of summer and he was returning the machinery to Mark's farm.

"Thanks for bringing it back in great shape," Mark said appreciatively, "I'm glad you got a third crop of hay out of your fields this year. You never know what God is going to provide each year so I'm thankful it worked out."

Mark consistently tried to bring God into the conversation with Leroy in an authentic way. They'd been neighbors for almost 20 years with little responsiveness from Leroy to talk about spiritual matters.

"Thanks again for letting me borrow it," Leroy responded. "I gotta fix the axle on my own cutter this winter." They shook each other's calloused hands. Leroy then got in his truck while Mark went back in the house where his wife was making lunch.

"How'd it go with Leroy?" she asked.

"Good, he brought it back with the blades sharpened," he replied. "He didn't want to talk about God again," Mark sat down in his chair for lunch. *"I just don't know what it'll take to break through to him about that stuff."*

Mark is being a faithful missionary to his neighbors. However, it might also be helpful for Mark to have a well rounded view of the Holy Spirit in regards to mission. The Holy Spirit is often the most misunderstood member of the trinity. This is unfortunate, because the Holy Spirit is essential for being an effective missionary! To illustrate this, J. I. Packer brilliantly writes:[8]

> *The Holy Spirit's distinctive new covenant role, then, is to fulfill what we may call a floodlight ministry in relation to the Lord Jesus Christ. So far as this role was concerned, the Spirit "was not yet" (John 7:39, literal Greek) while Jesus was on earth; only when the Father had glorified him (John 17:1, 5) could the Spirit's work of making men aware of Jesus' glory begin.*
>
> *I remember walking to a church one winter evening to preach on the words "he shall testify about me" (John 15:26), seeing the building floodlit as I turned a corner, and realizing that this was exactly the illustration my message needed.*
>
> *When floodlighting is well done, the floodlights are placed so that you don't see them; you are not in fact supposed to see where the light is coming from; what you are meant to see is just the building on which the floodlights are trained. The intended effect is to make it visible when otherwise it would not be seen for the*

---

8 J. I. Packer. *Keeping in Step with the Spirit: Finding Fullness in Our Walk with God*, 2nd ed. Grand Rapids, MI: Baker, 2005. 57.

darkness, and to maximize its dignity by throwing all its details into relief so that you see it properly. This perfectly illustrates the Spirit's new covenant role. He is, so to speak, the hidden floodlight shining on the Savior.

Or think of it this way. It is as if the Spirit stands behind us, throwing light over our shoulder, on Jesus, who stands facing us.

The Spirit's message is never,
> *"Look at me;*
> *listen to me;*
> *come to me;*
> *get to know me,"*
but always,
"Look at him, and see his glory;
> *listen to him, and hear his word;*
> *go to him, and have life;*
> *get to know him, and taste his gift of joy and peace."*

The primary job description of the Holy Spirit is to bring attention to the person and work of Jesus. This is especially important for mission because in order to be *fruitful* missionaries and not just *faithful* missionaries, we need to unshakably trust that the Holy Spirit will be the floodlight shining over the shoulders of our friends onto Jesus and, thus, bringing our friends to faith in Christ. Without the floodlight ministry of the Holy Spirit, nothing can bring soul-saving attention to Jesus. In light of this, it's extremely humbling to realize that all our innovative outreach strategies, all our clear gospel illustrations, all our faithful intentionality, and all our great spiritual conversations will never result in someone becoming a Christian if it's done in the absence of the floodlight ministry of the Holy Spirit.

Q1: In your own words, what's the role of the Holy Spirit in evangelism? How is this different than your role?

Q2: How does knowing this about the Holy Spirit affect the way you think about mission to your friends, neighbors, co-workers, and family members? How does it change what you pray about?

As J. I. Packer explained, the primary job description of the Holy Spirit is to bring attention to the person and work of Jesus. One of the passages in the Bible that clearly illustrates this is John 15:26–27:

> *When the Counselor comes, whom I will send to you from the Father, the Spirit of truth who goes out from the Father, he will testify about me. And you also must testify, for you have been with me from the beginning.*

In light of this passage, some of us are *Verse 26 People* and some of us are *Verse 27 People*.

Verse 26 People

These people genuinely trust the floodlight ministry of the Holy Spirit and his power to do the heavy lifting in salvation. They trust that no matter how diligent and wise their efforts are, their friends won't be brought to faith in Christ unless the Holy Spirit does the work that he promises (v. 26). However, even though these people eagerly trust the Holy Spirit, they might not take 15:27 seriously ("And you also must testify..."). Verse 26 People are generally eager to trust the Holy Spirit, but don't expect them to take serious risks for the sake of mission. They would much rather have the Holy Spirit do all the risk-taking for them and they wish that Jesus would have stopped talking at the end of verse 26.

Verse 27 People

These people aren't spiritual slackers. They know that their non-Christian friends are going to hell in a giant handbasket, and that bothers them. So they do their best. They strategize, prioritize, and evangelize. They know that what comes out of their mouth is important because faith comes through hearing the gospel (Romans 10:14–15). Even though they aren't perfect at verbalizing their faith, they still know that God can use them to reach their friends for Christ. They even have the bravery to pray and ask God for opportunities to share their faith! However, even though these people actually have the guts to take an evangelistic risk now and then, they might not take verse 15:26 seriously ("When the Counselor comes...he will testify about me"). Trusting the floodlight ministry of the Holy Spirit is an abstract concept to them, but trusting in themselves to try hard seems much more reasonable and practical.

Q3: Which one best describes you? Verse 26, Verse 27, a little bit of both, or neither? Why do you think this is?

 # WHEN YOU MEET

- Discuss the three questions in this chapter.

- In what way has your mindset changed after reading this chapter?

- In response to this chapter and your discussion, what is the Holy Spirit leading you to pray about together?

Simple Ideas for Mission

Below are four simple ideas for mission based on the average person's spheres of influence: where you live, where you work, where you play, and what your kids are involved in (if you don't have kids, feel free to ignore this one).

It's not practical or realistic to implement every idea below, so don't feel guilty for not being able to do it all. But even more importantly, we must remember that mission is something that should always stem from our identity in Christ. If it doesn't, then these ideas for mission will eventually feel burdensome and crushing. The gospel of belonging to Christ through faith in him is what gives our life value and worth, which is something that zeal for mission can never do. Start with the gospel, let it give you identity, and let it lead you to mission!

As a group, please read the simple ideas for mission below.

 WHERE YOU LIVE

Do you have a heart for your neighbors and do you feel the same way towards them that God does? Consider praying regularly that God will increase your heart for them and that he'll enable you to stay in step with the floodlight ministry of the Holy Spirit in your neighborhood.

WHERE YOU WORK

Make every effort to avoid spreading gossip and complaining at work. If you consistently avoid these traps over the course of several years, your co-workers will probably respect your character regardless of how close you are as friends. Earnestly pray that you'll be given opportunities to explain how Jesus is the one who affects your character, that it's not just you trying to be good and moral.

WHERE YOU PLAY

Consider being a regular at your favorite place to eat in town. Imagine if everyone in your church did this with the intentional purpose of being on mission. Over the long haul, what kind of conversations do you think you'd have through the floodlight ministry of the Holy Spirit?

YOUR KIDS

If you have little kids, consider taking them to "story time" at the public library. Not only will your kids enjoy it but the other parents and kids in attendance are probably going to be the same parents and kids that you're going to be crossing paths with over the next decade through school, clubs, sports, etc. Pray before you go that the Holy Spirit will be empowering you to get a jump-start on building these relationships for the sake of mission. Pray also that your relationship with them will be used in whatever way possible over the next decade to help bring them to Christ.

CHAPTER 4
PRAYING FOR
THE MISSION I

 **BEFORE YOU MEET**

"Timmy, we only go down the slides, not up them."

Becca had brought Timmy to a playdate at the park in their small town so she could have some adult conversation with her friend Jenny. Jenny's son Asher was now playfully chasing Timmy around the playground.

"You texted me about wanting to talk about small group last week?" asked Becca, finding a break in the action to start chatting.

"Yeah, thanks for reminding me about that!" Jenny exclaimed. "John and I were talking about it for over an hour after Timmy went to bed because the group discussion was amazing, but also a little frustrating."

"Really, why's that?" wondered Becca.

"Like I was saying to John, I feel like it's awesome that our group cares so much about being on mission to our neighbors and co-workers and we had a great discussion about how we need to prioritize praying about mission," *she explained.*

"*So what was the frustrating part?*" *asked Becca.*

"*I'm all for prioritizing it,*" *Jenny explained as she began to gaze past the playground.* "*I'm just confused about how to pray about mission besides just praying for a long list of people every day. I feel like there's more to it than that and I'm not sure what the Bible says about it.*"

"*Well, it probably says something about it...,*" *said Becca tentatively.*

Jenny brings up a great question: what does the Bible say about the connection of prayer and mission? Before we dive into specifics, let's briefly examine the nature of prayer and its connection to mission. On that topic, J. I. Packer insightfully writes:[9]

> *A hidden and deeply spiritual ministry of prayer is needed to back our evangelistic activity. God will make us pray before He blesses our labors in order that we may constantly learn afresh that we depend on God for everything. And then, when God permits us to see conversions, we shall not be tempted to ascribe them to our own gifts, or skill, or wisdom, or persuasiveness, but to His work alone, and so we shall know whom we ought to thank for them. Evangelistic fruitfulness will not come unless God also reforms our life of prayer.*

Q1: What stands out to you the most in this excerpt? Why?

---

9 J. I. Packer. "Isn't One Religion as Good as Another?" *Hard Questions*, ed. Frank Colquhoun. Downers Grove, IL: InterVarsity Press, 1977. 122–25.

Q2: How would you currently describe your prayer life in regards to mission?

Prayer Passages

For the most part, Christians know that prayer should be a key part of their mission. However, it's easy for us to get lost when it comes to understanding specifics of what *prayer* and *mission* should look like when they come together.

Numerous passages in the Bible about prayer can easily be applied to mission. For example, mission isn't the main point of the parable of the persistent widow in Luke 18, but it's perfectly fine to extract applications about mission from that passage, because we shouldn't give up praying for non-Christians. However, six passages in the New Testament talk about prayer in direct connection with mission. So let's do a brief study of these passages over the next two chapters.

> *After this the Lord appointed seventy-two others and sent them two by two ahead of him to every town and place where he was about to go. He told them, "The harvest is plentiful, but the workers are few. Ask the Lord of the harvest, therefore, to send out workers into his harvest field." – Luke 10:1–2*

In Luke 10, Jesus is surrounded by **seventy-two** followers who are eager to be on mission. Imagine if your church had seventy-two eager missionaries who were willing to do anything for the sake of reaching your small town with the gospel. You would probably just thank God for them, then tell them to get to work! But that's not what Jesus did. Before he sent them out, he instructed them to pray and **ask the Lord of the harvest to send out more workers**. Why did he tell them this? Among other reasons, seventy-two was apparently not enough. And it's also interesting that Jesus doesn't tell them to pray about the harvest, because he says it's already **plentiful**. Instead, the only thing he tells them to pray about is for God to send out more workers.

If you want mission in your small town to grow by *addition*, then you should simply pray for your own personal activity as a missionary. But if you want mission in your small town to grow by *multiplication*, then you should pray like Jesus tells his followers to do in this passage. God is the only one who has the power to make people into missionaries and send them. Do you pray this way about your neighborhood, your kids' schools, and your workplace? Do you pray for the houses that are for sale in your neighborhood, that God would send Christians to those houses that will be on mission with you to reach your neighborhood? Do you pray that God would send you Christian co-workers who will be on mission with you at the office? Do you pray for the annual hiring cycles at your kids' schools, that God would be sending Christian teachers, staff, and administrators so they can be on mission to reach their co-workers?

Keep in mind that the point of God sending missionaries to these places isn't to create safe Christian bubbles so that everyone can collectively hide their light under a bushel. The point is to multiply mission. God is in the business of transforming people into missionaries and sending them; that's why Luke 10:1–2 should be the *life verse* of anyone who is committed to the multiplication of mission in a small town.

Q3: What stands out to you in this passage in regards to praying about your mission?

Then they called them in again and commanded them not to speak or teach at all in the name of Jesus. But Peter and John replied, "Judge for yourselves whether it is right in God's sight to obey you rather than God. For we cannot help speaking about what we have seen and heard." After further threats they let them go. They could not decide how to punish them, because all the people were praising God for what had happened. For the man who was miraculously healed was over forty years old. On their release, Peter and John went back to their own people and reported all that the chief priests and elders had said to them. When they heard this, they raised their voices together in prayer to God. "Sovereign Lord," they said, "you made the heaven and the earth and the sea, and everything in them. You spoke by the Holy Spirit through the mouth of your servant, our father David:

'Why do the nations rage and the peoples plot in vain? The kings of the earth take their stand and the rulers gather together against the Lord and against his Anointed One.'

Indeed Herod and Pontius Pilate met together with the Gentiles and the people of Israel in this city to conspire against your holy servant Jesus, whom you anointed. They did what your power and will had decided beforehand should happen. Now, Lord, consider their threats and enable your servants to speak your word with great boldness. Stretch out your hand to heal and perform miraculous signs and wonders through the name of your holy servant Jesus." After they prayed, the place where they were meeting was shaken. And

> *they were all filled with the Holy Spirit and spoke the word of God boldly. – Acts 4:18–31*

This is a shocking passage because it goes against our common sense when our mission is confronted with a roadblock. Peter and John were **commanded** by the authorities **not to speak or teach at all in the name of Jesus**, which was a significant roadblock! If this happened to you, what would you do when you returned home to your friends? Would you passionately vent to each other? Would you get heated and angry? Would you fervently strategize your way around the roadblock? But Peter and John didn't do any of those things. They didn't spend their emotional energy on venting and strategizing; instead, they spent their energy on their knees. Prayer wasn't an afterthought—it was their first instinct when their mission was confronted with a roadblock. What's your first instinct when your mission isn't going well? Do you vent, strategize, or pray?

If that wasn't shocking enough, did you notice what they *didn't* pray about? They didn't pray that God would take away the roadblock! Instead the only thing they prayed about was for God to **enable** them with **great boldness** to advance the mission and for God to keep doing ministry through them. It seems like they were so consumed with the sovereignty of God and the needs of the mission that they simply forgot to pray for their comfort and circumstances.

After they prayed, they were **filled with the Holy Spirit and spoke the word of God boldly**. Since their prayer was for God to enable them with great boldness, it seems reasonable to infer that being filled with the Holy Spirit is strongly connected with their request to be enabled with boldness for their mission. Much ink has been spilled over what it means to be filled with the Holy Spirit. At the very least we must conclude from this passage that boldness for the sake of mission is not a by-product of natural talent and self-effort. Boldness is only produced and enabled by the Holy Spirit. What are you relying on to produce boldness:

an inspiring sermon, reading this book, or the power of the Holy Spirit?

Q4: What stands out to you in this passage in regards to praying about your mission?

 ## WHEN YOU MEET

- Discuss the four questions in this chapter.

- In what way has your mindset changed after reading this chapter?

- In response to this chapter and your discussion, what is the Holy Spirit leading you to pray about together?

Simple Ideas for Mission

Below are four simple ideas for mission based on the average person's spheres of influence: where you live, where you work, where you play, and what your kids are involved in (if you don't have kids, feel free to ignore this one).

It's not practical or realistic to implement every idea below, so don't feel guilty for not being able to do it all. But even more importantly, we must remember that mission is something that should always stem from our identity in Christ. If it doesn't, then these ideas for mission will eventually feel burdensome and crushing. The gospel of belonging to Christ through faith in him is what gives our life value and worth, which is something that zeal for mission can never do. Start with the gospel, let it give you identity, and let it lead you to mission!

As a group, please read the simple ideas for mission below.

WHERE YOU LIVE

Are there houses for sale in your neighborhood? Consider having your family and your small group pray that these houses will be sold to either a Christian who will be eager to be on mission with you in your neighborhood or to a non-Christian whom you can befriend and who is hungry for the gospel. Pray this in the hope that God will multiply mission in your neighborhood.

WHERE YOU WORK

Consider praying on a regular basis for the next round of hiring at your workplace. In addition to praying for new employees who do their job well, pray also that God will use this process to bring Christians who are eager to be on mission with you at work, as well as non-Christians whom you can easily connect with and who are spiritually open to the gospel.

WHERE YOU PLAY

If you were thinking about playing softball, horseshoes, or whatever else the Parks and Recreation department is offering this summer, consider starting or joining a city league team with your neighbors or co-workers along with a couple of other Christian friends who can be on mission with you. Sometimes spending time together outside of work or the neighborhood is necessary in order to have an effective gospel witness. But if your neighbors or co-workers aren't interested, pray your way through this minor roadblock and humbly ask God that he would enable you to speak the gospel to your friends with great boldness and in his timing.

♟ YOUR KIDS

If your kids go to public schools, pray regularly with your kids about their classmates and everyone's need for Jesus. Not only does this petition God for the salvation of their friends, but it also indirectly teaches them about the importance of mission at a young age and the necessity of prayer for the gospel to go forth.

CHAPTER 5
PRAYING FOR
THE MISSION II

 **BEFORE YOU MEET**

The honesty was flowing tonight at small group.

Teddy was leading the discussion and he was pretty nervous. The topic was about mission to their non-Christian friends, neighbors, and co-workers.

Kelly wasn't even sure if she cared about unbelievers and wasn't sure what to do about it. Matt admitted to being deeply fearful of rejection by people, which was on top of his fear of fumbling his words when talking about Jesus to his non-Christian friends. And it's true, Matt wasn't eloquent with words.

Roger seemed less concerned than Kelly and Matt. He confidently proclaimed that "whatever is going to happen is going to happen" and that mission is all about taking advantage of the opportunities when they come along, so "it's not worth getting bent out of shape about it." He added that praying is a great thing, but what he needed most was better training for training for how to share the gospel—because that's where the rubber actually meets the road.

Brandon followed that up by expressing his frustration that the group doesn't spend enough time praying about important things like revival and spiritual warfare as they relate to mission.

"Hopefully Scripture can give us some direction on all of this," Teddy hesitantly announced.

Teddy can rest assured that Scripture certainly does give us direction and insight to all of those questions. In this chapter we're going to finish our study of the six passages in the New Testament that talk about prayer in direct connection with mission.

Brothers, my heart's desire and prayer to God for the Israelites is that they may be saved. – Romans 10:1

Notice that Paul talks about his **heart's desire** in connection with his **prayer to God**. This is because the stuff we pray about is often an expression of the desires of our heart. That's why if we ever want to know what we truly care about, all we have to do is listen to what we pray about the most. The desire of Paul's heart was for people to **be saved**. Is that the desire of your heart? If your neighbor isn't a Christian, do you pour out your heart to God because you care about them? Are there non-Christians at your work or at your kids' school that you regularly pray for? Does your heart care enough to pray for them or does your heart easily drift towards apathy and indifference?

Did you know that the number-one killer of mission isn't bad doctrine or a lame outreach strategy? No, it's *apathy*. Don't get me wrong, bad doctrine or a lame outreach strategy will certainly immobilize your mission in various ways, but apathy will kill it faster than almost anything. That's because mission is murdered when our hearts are numb and don't truly care about the salvation of our neighbors and co-workers. If the desires of your heart are numb towards mission, I would suggest praying for God to change the desires of your heart because your heart is ultimately the problem, not your prayer life.

Q1: What stands out to you in this passage in regards to praying about your mission?

Pray also for me, that whenever I open my mouth, words may be given me so that I will fearlessly make known the mystery of the gospel, for which I am an ambassador in chains. Pray that I may declare it fearlessly, as I should. – Ephesians 6:19–20

Paul asked his friends to **pray also for me**, then he went on to detail how they could specifically pray for his mission. Stop right there. Did you see what Paul did? Paul, of all people, asked his friends to pray for his mission! If you know anything about Paul, he seems like the kind of guy who was naturally talented at sharing his faith and wasn't fearful at all when sharing the gospel. Paul realized that, even on his best day, he desperately needed his friends to pray for him and for the grace of God to empower his mission. Think of the most naturally talented evangelist in your church. Just like Paul, that man or woman is in desperate need of the grace of God and for others to pray for them. The same is true for us. What friends should you start sharing prayer requests with for the sake of your mission?

Paul goes on to ask his friends to pray that God would give him **words** to say **whenever he opens his mouth** to talk about **the mystery of the gospel** (Paul calls it a mystery because until this point people in the Old Testament didn't know when or under what circumstances Jesus was going to arrive). This is interesting because Paul's sermons in the book of Acts were phenomenal, he was an incredibly talented public speaker, and he was awesome at advancing the mission. But even with all his natural talent, Paul was convinced that he needed God to give him words whenever he opened his mouth to talk about the gospel. Paul knew that fruitful and effective words only come from God. This makes me breathe a sigh of relief because it's comforting to know that powerful and effective words don't come directly from my natural talent, but directly from the grace of God in response to prayer. This is good news for those of us who aren't naturally talented at sharing our faith.

Paul then twice asks his friends to pray that he would **fearlessly** declare and **make known** the gospel. The Greek word for fearlessly means "to have a free and fearless confidence" and it's the same Greek word that is used for boldness in Acts 4:29 (which we studied in the previous chapter). Proverbs 29:25 says, "Fear of man is a snare but whoever trusts in the Lord is kept safe." In this proverb, the fear of man is contrasted with trusting the Lord. Fear, in the biblical sense of the word, includes being afraid of someone but it also extends to holding someone in awe, being controlled or mastered by people, worshiping people, or using them for our personal sense of value, dignity, and worth. In other words, the fear of man can be summed up in five simple words—*we replace God with people*. Instead of fearing the Lord, we fear people.[10]

Think of if it this way: Jesus is the only one who should sit on the throne of your heart and mind. But when we fear people, somebody other than Jesus sits on that throne. Consequently, we care about that person's approval of us at least as much as much as God's approval. We want to please and appease them and we want them to never leave us nor forsake us. You know what that's called? Worship. That's because the most important relationship we have is with whoever sits on that throne.

---

10 Edward Welch. *When People Are Big and God Is Small.* Phillipsburg, PA: P&R Publishing, 1997. 14.

The fear of man will paralyze your mission because you can't witness to someone that you're trying to worship. Do you see how worship and mission are so deeply intertwined with each other? The most basic solution for the fear of man is the fear of the Lord. That's why, like Paul, we need friends who will pray for us to be fearless in our mission and have God as the only one competing for the throne of our heart and mind.

Q2: What stands out to you in this passage in regards to praying about your mission?

Devote yourselves to prayer, being watchful and thankful. And pray for us, too, that God may open a door for our message, so that we may proclaim the mystery of Christ, for which I am in chains. Pray that I may proclaim it clearly, as I should. – Colossians 4:2-4

Paul urges his friends to **devote** themselves **to prayer.** "Devote" is such an intense word! Would your closest friends say you're devoted to prayer? Keep in mind that being devoted to prayer isn't necessarily the same thing as being devoted to God, which is kind of like when someone is devoted to talking but doesn't pay attention to the person they're talking to. I think we all know people like that. If you ever do a brief study on how Jesus prayed you'll quickly notice that when he prayed he focused his attention on the Father. This is often in contrast with how many of us pray because we usually focus on prayer instead of the Father, which is kind of like focusing on the windshield when you're driving instead of focusing on the road. Those are the kind of people who cause accidents!

We're also to be **watchful** and **thankful** in the midst of being devoted to prayer. At the very least, being watchful and thankful is the opposite of going through the motions. Do you tend to go through the motions in life? If so, then you're probably going to miss lots of opportunities for mission. That's why it isn't a coincidence that Paul immediately proceeds to ask his friends to pray that God would **open a door** and provide opportunities for him to share the gospel. Is that the kind of request you ask your friends to pray for, or do you usually just ask them to pray for things like your Aunt Ethel's broken hip? I mean no offense towards Ethel or her hip, but are tragedies and physical health the only things we're called to pray for? Look at your church's prayer chain; I can almost guarantee that it's filled with prayer requests concerning tragedies and physical health. It's obviously good and right for us to pray for these things, but when was the last time your church's prayer chain overflowed with prayer requests like those in this passage? According to this passage, we are missing opportunities to share the gospel when we fail to pray for open doors. When it comes to prayer requests, are there imbalances like this that should we repent of?

Lastly, Paul asks his friends to pray that he would **proclaim** the gospel **clearly**. We **should** be eager to explain the gospel in a way that our non-Christian friends can understand. Unfortunately, many Christians talk about spiritual topics in a way that doesn't make sense to the average non-Christian. Often it's like we're speaking Klingon to them. This is unfortunate because almost no one understands Klingon except Klingons. Similarly, nobody understands Christian lingo and clichés except Christians. We also must conclude from this passage that clearly proclaiming the gospel is something that we should actively be praying about. This is crucial to remember because it's easy to think that the biggest reason why our mission isn't going well is because we don't know how to share our faith. While I certainly think that many of us would benefit from being better trained in how to share our faith, this passage leads us to believe that being trained will amount to nothing if we aren't devoted to praying.

Q3: What stands out to you in this passage in regards to praying about your mission?

Finally, brothers, pray for us that the message of the Lord may spread rapidly and be honored, just as it was with you. And pray that we may be delivered from wicked and evil men, for not everyone has faith. But the Lord is faithful, and he will strengthen and protect you from the evil one. – 2 Thessalonians 3:1-3

We should all concentrate on being faithful and patient missionaries in our workplaces, schools, and neighborhoods, because God hasn't placed us there by accident. In other words, we should focus on blooming where we're planted instead of grumbling and wishing we had a better job, a better neighborhood, and a better extended family. Faithfulness and patience over the long haul are vital to being a successful missionary in a small town. However, while faithfulness and patience are crucial to mission in a small town, in this passage we must also take note of Paul's holy dissatisfaction with his mission having such a small amount of fruit. This is what Paul means when he eagerly asks his friends to **pray** that the gospel would **spread rapidly and be honored**. He wants lots of people to become Christians, not just a few! What about you? Do you have a holy dissatisfaction with the amount of people becoming Christians in your town? If so, how is this reflected in your prayer life?

Paul then proceeds to ask his friends to pray that he would **be delivered from wicked and evil men**. We should certainly pray that people wouldn't hinder our mission, because the reality is that **not everyone has faith**. However, when we pray like this we also must keep in mind that wicked and evil men are not our enemies in the same way that Satan and demons are. That's why we should be watchful about our attitude towards people who are hindrances to our mission. Before we became Christians we were enemies of God just like they are, so we should resist the urge to label someone as a lost cause. Do we pray like Paul in this passage, or are we focused on trying to fix hindrances in our own strength?

Lastly, we would do well to avoid extremes when it comes to mixing spiritual warfare and mission. One extreme is to treat everything in your mission as having a strong demonic influence that must be actively and immediately addressed. The other extreme is to sweep the whole issue under the rug and treat demons like they don't have any meaningful influence on our mission. We would do well to imitate Paul when he balances his prayer request with the confident perspective that God **will strengthen and protect you from the evil one**. This is the type of confidence we should have when it comes to spiritual warfare, because our strength and protection comes from **the Lord**, because he **is faithful** to us and the advancement of his mission.

Q4: What stands out to you in this passage in regards to praying about your mission?

WHEN YOU MEET

- Discuss the four questions in this chapter.

- In what way has your mindset changed after reading this chapter?

- In response to this chapter and your discussion, what is the Holy Spirit leading you to pray about together?

Simple Ideas for Mission

Below are four simple ideas for mission based on the average person's spheres of influence: where you live, where you work, where you play, and what your kids are involved in (if you don't have kids, feel free to ignore this one).

It's not practical or realistic to implement every idea below, so don't feel guilty for not being able to do it all. But even more importantly, we must remember that mission is something that should always stem from our identity in Christ. If it doesn't, then these ideas for mission will eventually feel burdensome and crushing. The gospel of belonging to Christ through faith in him is what gives our life value and worth, which is something that zeal for mission can never do. Start with the gospel, let it give you identity, and let it lead you to mission!

As a group, read the simple ideas for mission below.

🏠 WHERE YOU LIVE

Consider going on a prayer walk around your neighborhood and using what you see as ideas for what to pray about. Pray for neighbors, kids, businesses, and especially for the advancement of the gospel all around town. Ask God to open your eyes and heart to see what he sees and to care what he cares about in your town.

💼 WHERE YOU WORK

Consider praying regularly with your spouse or your friends for the salvation of your co-workers and your risk-taking for sharing the gospel clearly and fearlessly at appropriate times. Do you pray that your co-workers would stop being annoying and start being moral and tolerable, or do you pray that they'll come to know Jesus and that he'll change them from the inside out?

📍 WHERE YOU PLAY

Do you leave your house in the evenings or do you consistently stay inside and keep to yourself? This may sound obvious but it's far too easy to sit in front of the television or endlessly explore the internet after a long day. We all need margin in our lives in order to be refreshed, but some of us are far too addicted to doing whatever is in our own best interests, night after night. Ask God to help you find the difference between relaxing and being self-centered with your time. What is he calling you to and how can mission be integrated into your life?

🧸 YOUR KIDS

Consider praying for the next rounds of hiring at the public schools such as teachers, aides, principals, administrative staff, librarians, and custodians, in the hope that the gospel would spread rapidly and be honored in the public schools. Pray that God will use this process to bring Christians that are eager to be on mission to the other teachers, aides, principals, staff, librarians, and custodians. That's because the best person to share the gospel with a teacher is another teacher. And the best person to share the gospel with a custodian is another custodian. Pray also that God will send non-Christian teachers, aides, principals, staff, librarians, and custodians whom God has been preparing to respond to the gospel. Pray that these new employees would quickly connect with Christians who work in their buildings and start building strong friendships that are conducive to them becoming Christians.

PART 3

THE MISSION AND SMALL TOWNS: ANALYZING CULTURE LIKE A MISSIONARY

CHAPTER 6
MISSION NEEDS ANALYSIS

 **BEFORE YOU MEET**

"I just don't like church people—well, except for you."

Doug and Luke were having a conversation while working on machines at the factory and it was nearing the end of their shift. Luke had become a Christian a couple years ago and Doug regularly expressed deeply rooted skepticism about matters of faith.

"What don't you like about church people?" Luke asked gently, being mindful of his tone so that he didn't sound defensive.

"Well," Doug started, *"they just seem fake, like they aren't real. Like the people I grew up going to church with. I don't know why people went there because they would just sing some songs, kneel to pray, go through the motions, then go home. It just never seemed authentic and it's not like people were ever interested in knowing who I was. I've found more authentic relationships here at work than I ever did at that church."*

"That sounds really frustrating," Luke said, at a loss for words.

"But you're different," Doug quickly added, *"because you ain't fake and you actually care about knowing people."*

It's worth noting that Doug sees and appreciates things about Luke that are important for doing mission well, namely authenticity and the priority of relationships. We'll explore these more in depth in this chapter, but first let's examine a couple of principles that are foundational to understanding mission anywhere.

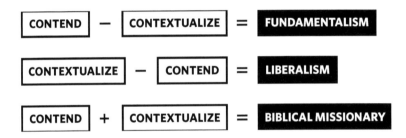

When it comes to deciding how to engage your small town with the gospel, you must think like a missionary and not just gravitate towards "what seems to work" or simply what you liked in your previous church. To adequately engage a culture with the gospel, every missionary needs to think in two categories: *contend* and *contextualize*.

Contend

> *Dear friends, although I was very eager to write to you about the salvation we share, I felt I had to write and urge you to contend for the faith that was once for all entrusted to the saints. – Jude 3*

Before we unpack this short passage, we need to clarify two points. First, when Jude says **the faith**, he is talking about the gospel. Scripture often refers to " the known and received body of truth about Jesus and salvation through him" in this way.[11] Second, when Jude says **saints**, he is referring to all Christians and not an elite group of spiritual people. This means that if you are a Christian, you are called to **contend** for the gospel—but what does that mean?

It means that contending is about the *message*.

It's about our passion for the gospel to be full, accurate, and not watered down, because it's an unchanging message for the salvation of all people, which includes everyone in your small town. It also means that we know the gospel so well that we can easily distinguish it from false forms of the gospel, kind of like someone who has eaten Kraft macaroni and cheese their whole life and knows when they're eating an imitation brand from Aldi. A missionary who takes Jude 3 seriously is someone who is deeply grieved when the gospel isn't proclaimed in its fullness, because this typically results in people being really confused about the nature and importance of the gospel and salvation.

Contextualize

Though I am free and belong to no man, I make myself a slave to everyone, to win as many as possible. To the Jews I became like a Jew, to win the Jews. To those under the law I became like one under the law (though I myself am not under the law), so as to win those under the law. To those not having the law I became like one not having the law (though I am not free from God's law but am under Christ's law), so as to win those not having the law. To the weak I became weak, to win the weak. I have become all things to all men so that by all possible means I might save some. – 1 Corinthians 9:19–22

---

11 Doug Oss and Thomas R. Schreiner. "Study Notes for Jude." *ESV Study Bible.* Wheaton, IL: Crossway, 2008. 2449.

If contending is about the *message*, contextualization is about our *methods*.

While Paul never went so far with his methods that he was sinning by neglecting the message, he had a strong passion to use **all possible means** to reach people with the truth of the gospel. While the central message of the gospel he preached never changed, he was flexible with the methods he used to proclaim it. This is what Paul means when he says, **I have become all things to all men so that by all possible means I might save some**. Every missionary contextualizes, whether they realize it or not. The only question is how good they are at it. For example, pretend that a missionary travels to a remote, unreached island to plant a church among native islanders. The missionary would be doing a bad job of contextualizing if he spoke English, wore a suit and tie, and explained that the substitution of Jesus on the cross is like Neo's role in the last scene of *The Matrix*. Conversely, the missionary would be doing a good job of contextualizing if he learned the native language, wore clothes that were appropriate to the island's culture, and explained the atonement in a way that the islanders would culturally understand.

There are countless examples of contextualization in small towns. Some examples would include the way we dress ourselves and our kids, the language and dialect we use, the size and shape of our church building, our standards for personal hygiene, our idiosyncrasies, how often we mow our lawn, the examples we use in our sermon illustrations, the amount of technology we use in our church services, and the illustrations we use to explain gospel concepts such as sin, atonement, repentance, and conversion to our friends and neighbors. And if we do a bad job of contextualizing there will be unnecessary barriers to our non-Christian friends getting saved.

To be a biblical missionary in a small town, we must have an equal zeal for contending and contextualizing. Unfortunately, many missionaries have a zeal for only one, which usually comes at the expense of our zeal for the other. When a missionary primarily contends but doesn't contextualize, that is usually the trap of fundamentalism. When a missionary primarily contextualizes but doesn't contend, that is usually the trap of liberalism. The key is to avoid both traps.

Q1: What is the difference between contending and contextualizing?

Q2: Why is it important for a missionary to have an equal zeal for contending and contextualizing?

Cultural Analysis

Now let's take a step back and examine one of the precursors to contending and contextualizing: *cultural analysis*.

> *Jews demand miraculous signs and Greeks look for wisdom, but we preach Christ crucified: a stumbling block to Jews and foolishness to Gentiles, but to those whom God has called, both Jews and Greeks, Christ the power of God and the wisdom of God. – 1 Corinthians 1:22-24*

The big picture in this passage is that Paul is doing cultural analysis so that he can identify the cultural idols of the people who live in the city of Corinth. That's what he's doing in verse 1:22 when he says that **Jews demand miraculous signs and Greeks look for wisdom.** Jews idolized pragmatism and power, which is why they would **demand miraculous signs.** Greeks—Paul's catch-all term for anyone who identified more with Greek and Roman culture than with Jewish culture—idolized the pursuit of philosophical ideas, which is why they would **look for wisdom.** But Paul chooses to **preach Christ crucified,** which sets the tone for the remainder of the passage because the gospel of Christ crucified confronts the idols of both Jews and Greeks. Paul then explains that Jews and Greeks respond differently to the preaching of the gospel. It was a **stumbling block** to the Jews because a crucified homeless guy doesn't sound like a powerful God to worship, or someone who could possibly be the Messiah (see Galatians 3:13), and it was **foolishness** to the Greeks because a crucified and resurrected god sounds like a foolish philosophical idea. He continues in verse 1:24 by explaining that the Jews and Greeks who become Christians **(but to those whom God has called)** are the ones who accept the confrontation of the gospel against their idols and, as a result, see Christ as Lord over their idols **(both Jews and Greeks, Christ the power of God and the wisdom of God).**

Paul thought that cultural analysis was a necessary part of being a missionary. And just like Paul, we should see this as an indispensable part of reaching our small town with the gospel. With that in mind, let's do some general cultural analysis below.

Q3: If Paul was writing 1 Corinthians 1:22 to your church, what would he say that the non-Christians in your small town demand or look for? For example, finish the following statement, "People in my small town look for _____?

A: Numerous insightful and valid answers could be given for this question that are specific to your small town. General answers could include comfort, family, love, security, purpose, etc. The list could go on and on, and I think there's some truth in all those answers. But one of the most universal and important answers to this question is relationships. People are starving for relationships whether they realize it or not. That's because all of us were made for this since we were made in the image of God who has eternally been in relationship as the Father, Son, and Holy Spirit. That's why so many of us desire to be married, have friends, and be in a family that's not dysfunctional. And that's one of the main reasons why so many of us love social networking, even in towns that are extremely rural. We long for relationships so that we can know and be known. And this longing inside us should point us back to the nature of the God who created us.

Q4: The last question zoomed in on your small town, now let's zoom out and look at American culture in general. Before the year 2000 , reality tv shows didn't exist for the most part, but now they dominate the landscape. Why do you think there are so many reality TV shows and what do you think this says about our culture?

A: One of the best answers is that people are desperately looking for authenticity. They are interested in what's real, not what's fake and scripted. That's primarily because the vast majority of us in America are marketed, pitched, and sold to every day of our lives. And this is especially true for younger generations. Therefore, we are a culture that is desperately looking for what seems authentic and real.

Q5: If our culture deeply values relationships and authenticity, how do you think this effects the way we do mission?

A: It seems reasonable to conclude that building relationships with non-Christians and living out our faith in an authentic way is foundational to having a well thought out and contextualized strategy for mission.

 **WHEN YOU MEET**

- Discuss the five questions in this chapter.

- In what way has your mindset changed after reading this chapter?

- In response to this chapter and your discussion, what is the Holy Spirit leading you to pray about together?

Simple Ideas for Mission

Below are four simple ideas for mission based on the average person's spheres of influence: where you live, where you work, where you play, and what your kids are involved in (if you don't have kids, feel free to ignore this one).

It's not practical or realistic to implement every idea below, so don't feel guilty for not being able to do it all. But even more importantly, we must remember that mission is something that should always stem from our identity in Christ. If it doesn't, then these ideas for mission will eventually feel burdensome and crushing. The gospel of belonging to Christ through faith in him is what gives our life value and worth, which is something that zeal for mission can never do. Start with the gospel, let it give you identity, and let it lead you to mission!

As a group, please read the simple ideas for mission below.

WHERE YOU LIVE

Offer to babysit your non-Christian neighbors' kids so they can have a date night. What a great way to care for your friends who aren't Christians! Pray that your authentic love and generosity will be an excellent reflection of the gospel to them.

WHERE YOU WORK

Consider visiting co-workers when they are in the hospital. You can even have your kids or grandkids make them get-well cards! It will probably speak volumes about how you authentically care for people. Visiting them means that you care about them as people and not just as co-workers.

📍 WHERE YOU PLAY

Don't constantly be staring at your phone or walking around with your earbuds in your ears. Although not inherently wrong, this can disconnect us from opportunities, big and small, to interact with others and to build the kind of relationships that can only be built through everyday interactions over the course of several years in your small town.

🧸 YOUR KIDS

If your kids go to public schools, treat your teachers like the experts they are. At conferences, ask good questions, take notes, and learn from them. Many parents don't attend conferences, so your mere attendance, not to mention your authentic eagerness to ask questions and learn from them, will probably speak volumes about your character. Pray in the weeks leading up to conferences that Christ would empower your light to shine for the sake of gospel advancement.

CHAPTER 7
COMMUNITY ON MISSION

 **BEFORE YOU MEET**

"That would totally screw up our small group."

Jason said this in the living room, while Andy and Ryan patiently listened but gently disagreed with him. Small group had ended an hour ago and the three guys were lingering while their wives chatted in the kitchen. Their disagreement was about inviting non-Christians into the group.

"It would just screw up how close we are and how deep we go as a group," he added.

"I don't see it that way," countered Andy. *"Depth and closeness haven't been sacrificed in the other small groups at church that have started inviting non-Christians. And all we would be doing as a group is authentically studying the Bible and praying together. I don't see where depth is sacrificed in that scenario."*

"And don't forget," added Ryan, *"people often need to belong before they believe. And I don't mean belonging in terms of church membership. I'm just talking about being*

purposefully included in a group like this. Seeing us authentically live out the gospel is the best apologetic for the gospel that I can think of."

Jason still wasn't sure. He needed some more time to think about it.

Many of us are like Jason because we often need time to thoughtfully reflect on how we integrate community and mission together. To that end, let's dive deeper into cultural analysis and its implications for how we do mission in small towns.

The Pyramid

Author and speaker Josh McDowell created the triangle diagram (see illustration).[12] McDowell says that for the last 500 years, people in our culture have had a predictable pattern for filtering through new ideas and adopting them into the fabric of their lives. He asserts that logic determined our beliefs, our beliefs determined our convictions, our convictions determined our values, and our values determined our behaviors. Logic was the most important aspect because it served as the chief entry point for the consideration of new ideas, such as the gospel.

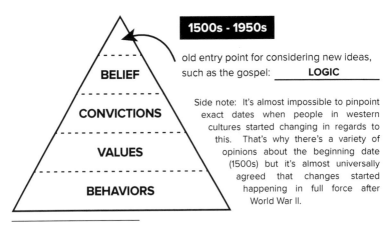

1500s - 1950s

old entry point for considering new ideas, such as the gospel: _____**LOGIC**_____

Side note: It's almost impossible to pinpoint exact dates when people in western cultures started changing in regards to this. That's why there's a variety of opinions about the beginning date (1500s) but it's almost universally agreed that changes started happening in full force after World War II.

BELIEF

CONVICTIONS

VALUES

BEHAVIORS

---

12 Josh McDowell. Winter Leadership Seminar. Milwaukee, WI. December 2004.

Since logic was the chief entry point, this helps explain why contact evangelism[13] was quite successful in previous generations (you could, generally, approach strangers and effectively appeal to their logic without needing to build a relationship with them that fostered trust). However, in the 1950s something started slowly changing at the top of the pyramid. Over time, logic was bumped down a step and replaced by a new chief entry point to our consideration of new ideas, such as the gospel. It's been bumped down by *relationships.*

This partially explains why contact evangelism isn't as effective as it was in previous generations. It's fair to say that contemporary generations tend to engage truth in the context of relationships even more so than previous generations. That's why doing relational evangelism is one of the best ways to contextualize the gospel.

Below are a few questions for you about relational evangelism.

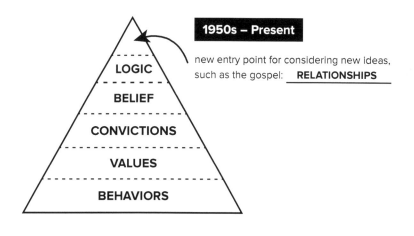

---

13 If you aren't familiar with these terms, "contact evangelism" is when you share the gospel with strangers and "relational evangelism" is when you share the gospel with friends, neighbors, and co-workers that you are building trust with over the course of time.

Q1: What are some advantages of doing relational evangelism as opposed to contact evangelism?

A: People tend to perceive who God is through the lens of their relationships with others. That's why it's generally ineffective to tell someone that God wants to have a personal relationship with them if you aren't interested in having a personal relationship with them. Relational evangelism also serves as a natural springboard for discipleship because relationships are essential for helping someone grow in Christ. After all, Jesus told us to make disciples (Matthew 28:16–20), which is starkly different than making superficial converts. And relational evangelism is an excellent strategy for small towns because mission in small towns often looks more like a crockpot than a microwave—which will be discussed in chapter 8.

Q2: What are some potential drawbacks to doing relational evangelism?

Q3: What can you do to avoid the potential drawbacks of relational evangelism?

A: To avoid these drawbacks, one of the most practical strategies is to be in close community with other believers. We need friends to ask us about our mission, pray with us about our mission, encourage us about our mission, and give us helpful advice about our mission. The power of our community should never be a substitute for the power of the Holy Spirit but one of the reasons we are called to be in community is to help "grease the wheels" of our mission. God designed community to be a means of grace to us and to the people we're witnessing to.

Community on Mission

A veteran ministry worker who has worked on university campuses in Wisconsin for three decades has made the following observation about how the landscape of mission has slowly been changing.[14] He said that when he was in college, a non-Christian would first have the gospel shared with them, then after they became a Christian they would join a Christian community. He said the process is still very similar today but the sequence of events is now in a slightly different order. Now a non-Christian first wants to join a Christian

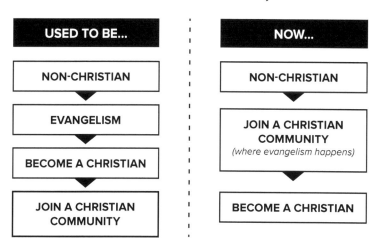

---

[14] InterVarsity Wisconsin West area team meeting in LaCrosse, WI in October 2007. The veteran ministry worker's name was Jay Anderson.

community, the gospel will be shared and lived out with them while they're a part of that community, then they eventually become a Christian. He said this pattern has been especially true over the last 15 years. Below is a visual representation of what he was saying.

Q4: In what ways is God calling you and your community of friends to build relationships with non-Christians, invite them into your community, and be bold in your witness to them?

A: Not only have these changes been happening on college campuses, but they've also been slowly happening with mission in our churches. Have you noticed this pattern? With the priority of relationships being at an all-time high, non-Christians are starving and seeking for a place to belong—before they believe.

 **WHEN YOU MEET**

- Discuss the four questions in this chapter.

- In what way has your mindset changed after reading this chapter?

- In response to this chapter and your discussion, what is the Holy Spirit leading you to pray about together?

Simple Ideas for Mission

Below are four simple ideas for mission based on the average person's spheres of influence: where you live, where you work, where you play, and what your kids are involved in (if you don't have kids, feel free to ignore this one).

It's not practical or realistic to implement every idea below, so don't feel guilty for not being able to do it all. But even more importantly, we must remember that mission is something that should always stem from our identity in Christ. If it doesn't, then these ideas for mission will eventually feel burdensome and crushing. The gospel of belonging to Christ through faith in him is what gives our life value and worth, which is something that zeal for mission can never do. Start with the gospel, let it give you identity, and let it lead you to mission!

As a group, please read the simple ideas for mission below.

WHERE YOU LIVE

Consider having a game night and cookout this summer where you invite all your neighbors (board games inside, yard games outside, activities for the kids, etc.). Invite your Christian friends from your small group, even if they don't live in your neighborhood, so they can build friendships with your neighbors who aren't Christians. And make sure to get on the same page with your Christian friends ahead of time so that this party has a deeper purpose than simply having fun.

💼 WHERE YOU WORK

Consider having your small group bring lunch to your workplace once a month for your department. Serving like this is not only a great way to care for your co-workers; it's also an easy springboard for discussions about community, church, Jesus, and other spiritual topics.

📍 WHERE YOU PLAY

Have a dessert and coffee night with one of your Christian friends from your small group and one of your friends who isn't a Christian. This is a great way to get out of the house, spend time with friends, build friendships with people who aren't Christians, and have fun eating and laughing. Pray about it ahead of time and have mission be a key motive of why you're doing it.

🧸 YOUR KIDS

Are you a mom with little kids who love to go to the park in the summer? Consider starting a regular play date and picnic a couple of times a month with other moms and their kids. Invite a few Christian friends from your small group and some non-Christian friends so you can be purposeful and on mission together instead of being a lone ranger.

CHAPTER 8
SMALL TOWNS ARE UNIQUE

 **BEFORE YOU MEET**

"I really like it, but it's just different in some ways."

Michelle and Karina were second-grade teachers in town. Today they were grading their second-quarter papers together in the empty teacher's lounge. They often chatted there and had gotten to know each other quickly from being on the same teaching team at school. They also went to the same church, which was a few minutes down the road. Michelle had just asked Karina how their town compared to the place where Karina had just moved from a few months earlier.

"I bet the grocery store is a lot less crowded than the big city you moved from," said Michelle.

"Yeah, but I think some of the differences go beyond just the population," Karina explained. "Even being a Christian is different in some ways, as weird as that sounds."

"What do you mean?" asked Michelle, as she leaned in with interest.

"Well," she answered, "in my last church they really emphasized that if you're a Christian then you're a missionary wherever you are, like here at school. I don't know how to put it into words, but there are just some things about living and working in this small town that confuse me when it comes to being a missionary."

"Tell me more about it," Michelle asked as she grabbed another stack of papers to grade.

Karina was on to something. Significant differences exist between small towns and larger cities when it comes to being on mission. Below are four factors that significantly affect mission in small towns. Some of these have a positive effect on mission; others, a negative effect. This list isn't comprehensive, but it's a good starting point for analyzing and discussing the unique factors that affect mission in a small town.

Factor #1: Religious Non-Christians

Not many people in small towns are atheists, Muslim, or new agers. Instead, small towns tend to be loaded with religious non-Christians. They may not go to church very often, but they generally believe that God exists and the Bible probably has something to say about him. Small towns tend to attract and retain people who are more traditional in their outlook on life compared to those in larger cities.

Religious non-Christians are generally receptive to talking about God and church but it's fair to say that they are also inoculated against the gospel. When a person is inoculated they receive a vaccine that is a weak strain of a virus. The body's immune system then proceeds to adapt so that when it comes in contact with the real strain of the virus, it can easily fight it off. Similarly, religious non-Christians grow up in churches that give them a weak strain of the gospel and, consequently, they build up an immunity to the real gospel. That's why conversations with them about the gospel and faith often end with them nodding their head in agreement with everything you say, even though they don't truly understand what you're talking about.

PRACTICAL ADVICE

Mission can never be done in the absence of prayer, but you'll especially realize this when you're on mission to religious non-Christians in a small town. Patience, taking a long-term approach to mission, is important. You won't typically see many "microwave" conversions among religious non-Christians; instead, you'll usually see "crockpot" conversions because it typically takes a long time for them to realize they have a weak strain of the gospel. But take heart, because the Holy Spirit is sovereign over the crockpot! This is why it's wise to avoid relying too much on short presentations of the gospel. More often than not, mission among religious non-Christians takes extended examinations of the lordship of Christ and the nature of the gospel before those concepts start to click in a meaningful way. This is why you should consider inviting people to your church, your small group, or to go through an extended one-on-one or couple-to-couple evangelistic Bible study. As we discussed in chapter 7, people are often starving for a place to belong before they believe. This *belonging* kind of environment should be a safe place for religious non-Christians to enter into community and see—up close and personal—how their weak strain of the gospel contrasts with the power and abundant life of the true gospel.

Religious non-Christians also tend to have a high regard for the Bible. That's why they're generally not freaked out by opening the Bible at church, reading it in small group, or talking about it casually. However, even though they have a high regard for the Bible, the vast majority of them don't know what it says because they've rarely been encouraged to read it for themselves. Therefore, don't be afraid to conversationally use Scripture to discuss the gospel and faith. You'll be surprised at how effective this is!

Factor #2: Change and Conformity

For a variety of reasons, people in small towns are not typically open to change in comparison to people who live in larger cities. But this isn't necessarily bad, because when people actually do change, they aren't likely to change back to their old ways. This is often the case when someone becomes a Christian in a small town: they aren't likely to turn their back on Jesus after they've switched their allegiance to him. Similarly, the lack of change in small towns often leads to a high degree of conformity. For better or worse, there is a relatively narrow range of acceptable behaviors, choices, and ideas that people are generally expected to adhere to in a small town. And the smaller a town is, the narrower the range! For people who have odd personalities or embrace non-traditional behaviors, it's often difficult to be respected in the goldfish bowl of a small town. In fact, Christians like this might even have a reputation that is ultimately at odds with their mission.

PRACTICAL ADVICE

A veteran pastor in a small town once told me, "You can't be weird in a small town. You need to be normal. You can't scare people and expect to advance the gospel. You can maybe get away with being weird in Seattle or Chicago and still be great at evangelism but that doesn't work in a small town."[15] If you think this might describe you, I would suggest talking with your pastor or a trusted friend and get their advice so that mission can advance your spheres of influence.

Factor #3: Reputations Are Hard to Shake

It's often said that newspapers in small towns don't *report* the news, they *confirm* the news. That's because people know who

---

[15] Private conversation in October 2013 with Pastor Stuart Dix from The Village Church in Baldwin, WI.

you are and there are parts of your life that are common knowledge around town (which wouldn't be the case in a larger city). In fact, many people who live in small towns end up being celebrities without trying, and for all the wrong reasons. Even your police record will be common knowledge because all the citations are listed in the newspaper! For better or worse, people tend to know about the details and integrity of your marriage, family, and business. That's why reputations are hard to shake in small towns and they tend to follow us around like our shadows.

PRACTICAL ADVICE

Again, for better or worse, the reputation of the gospel is strongly tied to the reputation of our marriage, family, and business. This is especially true in a small town. This reality can be a helpful asset to your mission, or an incredible liability. If you are committed to being on mission in your town, it might be helpful to sit down with your pastor or a trusted friend and reverse-engineer your marriage, family, and business. In other words, if you want the reputation of your marriage, family, and business to point to the gospel, then you'll need to decide on the series of steps you may need to take to make that happen. However, as you go through this process, don't accidentally make your reputation into an idol. If you do, you probably won't take meaningful risks for the gospel, because your deepest desire will be to protect your reputation instead of advancing the mission.

Factor #4: The "Ten and Done" Principle

A veteran pastor in a small town made a simple but insightful observation to me a few years ago about relationships in small towns. He called it the "ten and done" principle, and it forever changed the way I understood social dynamics and mission in small towns.[16]

The "ten and done" principle is when people in a small towns typically make room for ten slots in their life for friendships, and once their ten slots are filled, then they are done building friendships. They aren't necessarily done being friendly, but they are done inserting new friends into their slots. Each person's slots consist of permanent and non-permanent friendships.

The permanent slots are friendships that are poured in cement. These permanent friendships usually consist of a person's family, a few friends they grew up with, or other people they've grown close to along the way. The non-permanent slots may rotate depending on circumstances and stage of life. For example, when a young mom has little kids she might have some of the young moms from her play group in some of her non-permanent slots. However, when her kids are older and play on a high-school soccer team, she might have different parents in her non-permanent slots from that group.

Keep in mind that this is only a principle, and not a rule, because it's not equally true for everyone who lives in a small town. Some people might have a meager amount of non-permanent slots while others might have an abundance of them. Some might have considerably more than ten slots but they're all permanent, while others might have far less than ten slots, due to their personality and social sensibilities. Moreover, the cultural climate in some parts of the country can breed unspoken expectations for people to have higher or lower amounts of slots. But even though each person and place is different, the "ten and done" principle generally holds true for small towns across America. Many of us who have lived in small towns have certainly seen it in practice!

---

[16] Private conversation in November 2012 with Pastor Jeff Nettles from Rolling Hills Church in Platteville, WI.

PRACTICAL ADVICE

The "ten and done" principle creates a diversity of challenges when it comes to mission in small towns. If relationships are the foundation of mission in small towns, how should we do mission with this principle in mind? Below is a collection of thoughts that address this question.

- New people tend to be the "low-hanging fruit" for mission in a small town, because not many of their slots are filled. Longtime residents need the gospel as much as anyone, but new residents are often the easiest people to connect with for the sake of mission.
- Make room for non-permanent slots in your life for the sake of mission. If you don't have non-permanent slots open, take account of your relationships and ask God how he wants to organize and prioritize your friendships. If you do have non-permanent slots open, be devoted to praying about which non-Christians God might place in your slots.
- Don't assume you know which non-Christians have non-permanent slots open. Be prudent in praying for wisdom and don't jump to conclusions about who's interested and available to build a reciprocal friendship with you.
- For a variety of reasons, people who are single typically have more time and availability than their married counterparts. And they also tend to have a higher number of slots available than those who are married. Singles often have the potential to be some of the best missionaries in town. If you are single, consider leveraging this season of your life for the sake of mission.
- The "ten and done" principle often means that being on mission at our workplaces is remarkably strategic. Many people in small towns have their extended families living in the area and they fill up each other's slots. Consequently, some extended families in small towns could virtually be considered unreached people groups! One of the most strategic

ways to reach these families is to be on mission in our workplaces, because people from these families are forced to be around their Christian co-workers for eight hours every day.

- Some non-Christians have all their permanent slots filled with family and childhood friends. Therefore, consider strategically praying that God would boldly bring individual people like this to Christ so that they can be on mission to the rest of their family and childhood friends. This is one way that God infiltrates closed networks of family and friends in small towns. There are many people in small towns who have testimonies where God saved them and powerfully used them to reach their closed network of family and friends. Let's pray that this would happen more often!

- If your family takes up all your slots and they are already Christians, consider holding a family-wide discussion about what doing mission in your town should look like. Family is good and a blessing from God, but is your family's mission focused on community with each other or are you a community that's focused on mission?

Q1: What are the two to three things that stood out to you in the list of factors? Why did they stand out to you?

Q2: What are some factors that effect mission in your town that you would add to the list?

 # WHEN YOU MEET

- Discuss the two questions in this chapter.

- In what way has your mindset changed after reading this chapter?

- In response to this chapter and your discussion, what is the Holy Spirit leading you to pray about together?

Simple Ideas for Mission

Below are four simple ideas for mission based on the average person's spheres of influence: where you live, where you work, where you play, and what your kids are involved in (if you don't have kids, feel free to ignore this one).

It's not practical or realistic to implement every idea below, so don't feel guilty for not being able to do it all. But even more importantly, we must remember that mission is something that should always stem from our identity in Christ. If it doesn't, then these ideas for mission will eventually feel burdensome and crushing. The gospel of belonging to Christ through faith in him is what gives our life value and worth, which is something that zeal for mission can never do. Start with the gospel, let it give you identity, and let it lead you to mission!

As a group, read the simple ideas for mission below.

WHERE YOU LIVE

Do you ever get frustrated or impatient with neighbors who are religious non-Christians because they just don't seem interested in changing? In these situations, pray that you would remember "common grace." Common grace is a theological phrase that means that God is at work in the lives of non-Christians whether they realize it or not. For example, Jesus says that the Father "causes the sun to rise on the evil and the good and sends rain on the righteous and the unrighteous" (Matthew 5:45). This is just one small example of how God is at work in their lives. Be encouraged that God loves religious non-Christians enough to not only send them the sun and rain but also to send Christians on mission into their lives so that they can come to Christ. Trust God that he is at work and is on mission with you for his glory and their good.

WHERE YOU WORK

Seek first to understand before you seek to be understood. Many of our opinions about people and situations at work are based on partial information, inaccurate information, or wrong assumptions. Before you come to a conclusion or an opinion about anyone or anything, seek first to understand by asking tactful questions with a teachable spirit. If this is done with humility, it will probably set you apart as a person of character among your non-Christian co-workers. This can only serve to enhance your testimony and point people to the gospel.

● WHERE YOU PLAY

Obey the traffic laws, stop for people in the crosswalk, don't make gestures with your hands when someone cuts you off, and don't pull out in front of people when you're in a hurry. You live in a small town where people know who you are, where you live, what car you drive, and where you go to church. Make sure to drive in a way that doesn't accidentally short-circuit your reputation and mission.

🧸 YOUR KIDS

Pray regularly with your spouse or a trusted friend for the salvation of your family members who aren't Christians. Pray also that your kids will trust and follow Christ so that they can have a generational impact on their cousins and peers for the sake of mission. Ask God for perspective and trust God to do his work.

PART 4

THE MISSION AND INTENTIONALITY: BEING INTENTIONAL LIKE A MISSIONARY

CHAPTER 9
EXPLORING INTENTIONALITY

 **BEFORE YOU MEET**

"Kick the ball, Kenny...go get it!"

Kim joyfully screamed this as Kenny zig-zagged up and down the soccer field on a brisk Saturday morning in their small town. A flock of parents checkered the sidelines, with most cheering for their kids just as fervently.

Kim was thankful for something fun to do on a Saturday morning because it was a good break in the daily grind of being a single mom. But this game was a little different than the others. Her small group had recently talked through a list of questions. One especially stuck with her: What did she think about mission in the different parts of her life, like Kenny's soccer game?

"Keep it up, Kenny...you're doing great!"

She glanced over at the flock of parents in between her yells of encouragement as she continued to reflect.

How many of these parents, she wondered, are followers of Christ? How many of them do I know? How many have I tried to get to know at games and practices this season?

"The ball is going the other way...you can do it!"

Do I know any of these parents from other places in town? Wait, did I even pray about talking to anyone before I came here? Do I actually want to get to know any of these people?

"You're here for a reason, Kenny...go get 'em!"

Kim is starting to ask the right questions and that's the best place to begin. In light of that, this chapter is filled with questions that are designed to help you think about mission in your town. Like the questions and ideas we've been thinking and praying through at the conclusion of every chapter up to this point, they focus on mission in four spheres: *where we live, where we work, where we play,* and *what our kids are involved in.* They are designed to help you process and explore how to naturally incorporate mission into the existing spheres of your life.

Many of us balk at the idea of adding mission to our lives because our schedule is already so full. However, most of us don't need to add more stuff to our schedule in order to be on mission. Instead, most of us simply need to pray and be intentional in the spheres of influence God has already given us.

Pray and ask for the Holy Spirit to lead you as you process the questions on the following pages.

Sphere of Influence #1: Where You Live

- Who are your neighbors and what do you know about them spiritually?

- What kind of reputation do you have in your neighborhood? What factors or events have led to the forming of your reputation? If you want to be on mission, what kind of reputation should you have in your neighborhood?

- How often do you pray for your neighbors and what do you pray about? Who should you be praying with about these things?

- What houses and apartments are coming up for sale or rent in your neighborhood? What kind of things would be good to pray about in this regard?

- How much do you love your neighbors? Why do you think this is?

- Is your home known as a place of hospitality in your neighborhood? If not, what do you think is holding you back from being on mission through hospitality?

- What are three simple things you can do to be more intentional about building relationships with your neighbors that would lead to mission?

Sphere of Influence #2: Where You Work

- Who are your co-workers and/or clients and what do you know about them spiritually?

- What kind of reputation do you have at work? What factors or events have led to the forming of your reputation? If you want to be on mission, what kind of reputation should you have at work?

- How often do you pray for your co-workers and/or clients? What do you pray about? Who should you be praying with about these things?

- Are there other Christians that you work with? Are you on mission together or are you all just "trying hard, earning paychecks, and going through the motions"? What do you think it would look like to be on mission together?

- How much do you love your co-workers and/or clients? Why do you think this is?

- Do your co-workers and/or clients think you're interested in getting to know them? Why do you think this is?

- If Jesus had your job, what kind of risks would he take for the sake of the mission?

Sphere of Influence #3: Where You Play

- What activities are you personally involved in? (e.g., clubs, teams, groups, organizations, etc.

- How are these activities potential springboards for mission?

- What are you praying about in regards to integrating mission with your activities? Who else is committed to praying with you about this?

Sphere of Influence #4: Your Kids

- What activities are your kids involved in (including school)?

- How do you see these activities as a potential springboard for mission?

- What are you praying about in regards to integrating mission with your kids' activities? Who else is committed to praying with you about this?

Bonus Questions

- In what ways does your mission in any of these spheres overlap? What are some benefits of these spheres overlapping?

- Who are some Christian friends that you should invite into these spheres to be on mission with you? Why do you think there is value to being on mission together in these spheres instead of being a lone ranger?

WHEN YOU MEET

- Have each person in your group share answers to three or four questions.

- In what way has your mindset changed after reading this chapter?

- In response to this chapter and your discussion, what is the Holy Spirit leading you to pray about together?

CHAPTER 10
SIMPLE IDEAS
FOR MISSION

 **BEFORE YOU MEET**

"But what does that mean for us?"

Kaitlin was asking Dustin some good questions on the ride home after small group. The group had just finished discussing and praying about being on mission in the normal, everyday parts of life.

"I feel like everyone in that group focuses on the big picture," she continued. "I'm just more practical so discussions like that make me feel frazzled." Dustin slowed down and stopped at a red light.

"I can't believe they put a traffic light here. This town didn't need another stop light," he remarked. "Wait, why did you say you're frazzled?"

"Yeah, it's nothing personal or anything," she said as she stared out the window. "Sometimes I just get overwhelmed when our group talks about being on mission. It just feels so overwhelming. I want to follow Jesus and be on mission with

him here in town but I just don't think I have time to add it to our schedule."

"I can't believe this light is still red, there's no traffic in sight," said Dustin, as he tried to wait patiently. "And I hear what you're saying, honey. I think our group could definitely be more practical, but I also don't think we need to necessarily add anything to our schedule. I think it's more about being intentional with the stuff in life that we're already doing."

As he said this, the light turned green.

Like many of us, Kaitlin thinks mission should be practical. This chapter will offer several simple ideas for mission that are categorized by the four spheres of influence from the previous chapter. For those of you who get easily overwhelmed, you may already be breathing into a paper bag in anticipation of reading this list. Let me ease your anxiety: it's not practical or realistic to implement every idea in this chapter so don't try doing everything!

Even more importantly, as I've said in each chapter above, we must remember that mission is something that should always stem from our identity in Christ. If it doesn't, then these ideas for mission will probably and eventually feel burdensome and crushing. The gospel of belonging to Christ through faith in him is what gives our life value and worth, which is something that zeal for mission can never do. Start with the gospel, let it give you identity, and let it lead you to mission!

When reading this list, notice how the majority of the ideas are about connecting prayer and intentionality to what you're already doing. Less than half involve any significant rearranging of your schedule. But don't fight the leading of the Holy Spirit if God is calling you to rearrange your schedule to align more with mission in your small town.

Please read the following ideas and answer the questions at the end.

Sphere of Influence #1: Where You Live

IDEA #1   *Play with your kids in the front yard instead of the back yard (or whichever yard where you usually have the most interaction with your neighbors). Make it a habit to briefly pray before you go outside about any non-Christians that God would have you interact with that day.*

IDEA #2   *Do your best to avoid spreading and listening to gossip in your neighborhood. If your witness is a jigsaw puzzle, your character is a corner piece—a vital place to start building from.*

IDEA #3   *Ask longtime residents in your neighborhood to help you learn about the history of the neighborhood, as long as it doesn't turn into gossip. You'll probably hear lots of great stories and it's a great way to build relationships with your neighbors who aren't Christians. If you are a longtime resident in your neighborhood, what are you doing and praying about in order to cultivate a witness for the gospel in your neighborhood?*

IDEA #4   *If you have any specialized skills or tools, then allow your neighbors use of them, free of charge. Pray that people will take you up on your offer and that the Lord will use your willingness for the advancement of the gospel in your neighborhood.*

IDEA #5   *Lead a coat or food drive this winter in your neighborhood. In addition to helping people in need, this might be a great way to build relationships with some of your non-Christian neighbors.*

IDEA #6   *Hand out the best treats in the neighborhood during Halloween. Also, go door to door with your kids and introduce yourself to your neighbors if you haven't already met them. Ask God ahead of time to bless your efforts with your neighbors this Halloween.*

IDEA #7   *If there are elderly people in your neighborhood, organize your neighbors to help care for them in simple ways. Not only is this a great way to help people in your neighborhood, but it's also an easy way to connect with neighbors who aren't Christians.*

IDEA #8   *If people in your neighborhood are environmentally conscious (or even if they're not!), start a neighborhood compost pile that everyone can use. Have it on your property and pray that it would be an easy way to connect with your non-Christian neighbors on a regular basis this summer.*

IDEA #9   *Consider delivering baked goods (e.g., fresh bread, cookies, or brownies) to the college students, single people, and families with little kids who live around you. Be sensitive to their dietary concerns. Pray that God will use your love and hospitable acts to build relationships with people who aren't Christians.*

IDEA #10   *Have an Easter egg hunt in your back yard and invite your friends and neighbors who aren't Christians. Invite your Christian friends so that they can network and build relationships with everyone as well.*

IDEA #11   *Create a neighborhood email and phone contact list for safety in case anyone sees anything that's troubling or illegal in the neighborhood. This would also serve as an easy way to casually stay in contact with your neighbors and have something in common to discuss.*

IDEA #12 If your neighbors are going through a stressful time or have a time of need, eagerly volunteer to watch their kids. If you're comfortable with it, let them do the same for you. Often one of the best ways to build a relationship with someone is by letting them serve you.

IDEA #13 Host a kids' movie night for kids in the neighborhood. If you're retired or empty-nesters, this is a great way to steward your time in this stage of life for mission! Doing this should help you build rapport with your friends and neighbors who aren't Christians.

IDEA #14 Grow extra produce in your garden this summer so that you can share the extras with your friends and neighbors who aren't Christians. Pray that God will empower your efforts to build these relationships.

IDEA #15 If you go walking or running on a regular basis, start a group among the other walkers/runners in your neighborhood. This is a simple way to use your regular routine to get to know your neighbors better.

Sphere of Influence #2: Where You Work

IDEA #16 Pursue excellence in your field of work. Your co-workers, supervisors, and clients will respect your work ethic long before they respect what you think about the gospel. However, this pursuit shouldn't create an imbalance your life. Pursue excellence, maintain life balance, and avoid being a perfectionist, not just so that you can be in line for a raise or a promotion, but to give credibility to the gospel.

IDEA #17   *If your co-workers know you're a Christian, ask God about simple things you can do in your workplace to tactfully align yourself with Jesus. Talk this over with a trusted friend or your pastor, just to make sure you don't do anything crazy that would be counter-productive to the advancement of the gospel in your workplace.*

IDEA #18   *Strive for integrity with everything you do. When you identify yourself with Jesus, people are going to be watching you like a hawk. But don't get frustrated or stressed out. Allowing your character and integrity to shine in the workplace is a phenomenal long-term strategy for mission. People often want to experience a living example of something before they'll want to consider it themselves.*

IDEA #19   *Work hard to reconcile co-workers who are at odds with one another. Be prayerful and tread lightly, depending on the complexities of the situation. Helping people reconcile is an art and, if done well, can point to the reality that reconciliation is a value that God cares about so deeply that he sent his son to die so that we could be reconciled to him. Also, temper your approach because we shouldn't expect non-Christians to act like they're Christians. As always, seek wise counsel from your pastor or a trusted friend first.*

IDEA #20   If you are a small business owner, organize a group for local entrepreneurs at a coffee shop in town. In addition to helping your business (and the coffee shop) flourish, pray and ask God how he would have you appropriately leverage this group for mission.

IDEA #21   Invite your co-workers over for dinner. Someone who's reading this might object by saying, "I don't like my co-workers enough to invite them into my house." That reminds me of what Jesus said, "If you love those who love you, what credit is that to you? Even 'sinners' love those who love them. And if you do good to those who are good to you, what credit is that to you? Even 'sinners' do that" (Luke 6:32–33). As you do this, ask God to bless you as you move out of your comfort zone.

IDEA #22   If it's suitable for your workplace, find out your co-workers' favorite music and make a playlist. Pray that God would help you appreciate the musical preferences of your co-workers. Flexibility and forbearance are important for the sake of mission and are hallmarks of spiritual maturity.

IDEA #23   Make every effort to know the names of all your co-workers and clients along with their families and other relevant information about them. If you need to, make a list of this information. You may feel a little weird to be this deliberate about it, but if you care deeply about knowing someone, you should be willing to do anything in order to remember important things about them. Remembering important information helps build trust which, in God's timing, will hopefully lead to them giving their lives to Christ.

IDEA #24   *Take initiative and be the first person to greet and welcome new people at work who have just been hired. If they just moved here with their family, they most likely don't know anyone in town and might be starving for friendships and community sooner rather than later. Co-workers that are new to the area are often some of the most fruitful people to invest our time and energy with. God often uses new surroundings and circumstances to bring us to faith in him. What are you praying about in regards to your new co-workers that will be hired over the next year?*

IDEA #25   *Do you struggle with your attitudes and actions towards your supervisor and co-workers? Only God can change us deeply, but we must pray and trust God to change us while also taking action ourselves. Come up with a list of personal core values for how to conduct yourself at work and how to interact with co-workers. Work through this list with your pastor or a trusted friend. It's incredibly valuable for non-Christians at your workplace to see a man or woman of God who is willing to be humble and change over the course of time.*

IDEA #26   *Don't just build relationships with the other Christians at work. Your co-workers who aren't Christians are there to be loved and noticed as well. You might be one of the only Christians that your co-workers and/or clients have ever met, or the one they know the best. How should this change what you pray about?*

IDEA #27   *Eagerly offer to cover for co-workers who might need time off of work. The key words are eagerly and offer. If you do this with the attitude of a servant, your co-workers will probably respect you. This is the kind of person whose testimony about the gospel is taken seriously by their co-workers.*

IDEA #28   *When possible, carpool to work with one of your non-Christian co-workers. Not only would this save gas money but it would also allow you to build a good friendship with them and eventually have quality spiritual conversations when you're trapped in the car together.*

IDEA #29   *Pray for your co-workers during your commute. If you have an extremely short commute, arrive at work a few minutes early so you can spend some time praying. Among other things, pray for your witness to your co-workers and/or your clients.*

IDEA #30   *Start and lead a lunchtime Bible study at your work for your co-workers who aren't Christians. Evangelistic lunchtime Bible studies at work are often some of the most strategic places to reach out to non-Christians. Set up a meeting with your pastor to talk through what this might look like for your workplace and how to pitch this idea to your supervisor and how to recruit for it.*

Sphere of Influence #3: Where You Play

IDEA #31   *Start a sewing club that meets two or three times per year. Start out with four of your Christian friends who are committed to making this a ministry instead of simply a time to sew. Prayerfully consider how to advertise the group as well as how to make it a place where people who aren't Christians feel loved and cared for.*

IDEA #32 *Join organizations like the Rotary Club, not just because you love your town and to network for your business, but also because it's a great way to meet people that you'd probably never meet otherwise. It's okay to network with people for a variety of reasons, but your networking should never come at the expense of Jesus and his kingdom.*

IDEA #33 *Host a ladies' craft night with an intentional mix of friends who are Christians and non-Christians. Pray beforehand and remember to ask your Christian friends to take the initiative to get to know your non-Christian friends at the event, since relationships are an essential foundation to mission in a small town.*

IDEA #34 *Waiters and waitresses know who you are. Seriously. They also know who is generous and who isn't, especially in a small town. If you go out to eat, budget for a generous tip. If giving an extra couple dollars as a tip will enhance and protect the reputation of the gospel, then that's a great investment! The last thing we want to see is our non-Christian server at church thinking, "Ugh, there's that lousy tipper! I bet this whole room is full of people like that." Also, how much does your tipping reflect the gospel? Tip generously, even when your servers don't appear to be very good at their jobs that day and don't seem deserving of such generosity. God was more than generous to us when he died for us, and we didn't exactly deserve that either.*

IDEA #35   *If you regularly go to the gym to work out, go there at the same time of day, so you can get to know the other regulars. Also, consider not using earbuds when working out, since it's hard to be approachable when you're listening to music. Ask God each time you go to provide opportunities for you to connect with whomever he wants you to.*

IDEA #36   *What's your favorite hobby? Start a local club that meets a few times a year so you can develop friendships and enjoy your hobbies with people you might never meet otherwise. Recruit a Christian friend to be in the group so you can pray together and integrate mission and intentionality into the group.*

IDEA #37   *Don't ever be rude or nitpicky with a waiter or waitress, because you will get a reputation quickly. Reputations are built quickly, die slowly, and follow us like our shadows do.*

IDEA #38   *Host a Pampered Chef, Mary Kay, or Twenty-One party. Invite Christian and non-Christian friends, co-workers, family members, and neighbors that you think you would connect well with. Events like these usually have great potential for mission because they typically serve as an easy entry point for women to feel known and connected.*

IDEA #39   *Throw a Fourth of July party that's purposefully rooted in mission. Invite both your Christian and non-Christian friends so they can get to know each other. Pray ahead of time so that your mission doesn't rely on self-effort and your ability to plan.*

IDEA #40   *Learn to ask good questions in conversations with people you meet around town who aren't Christians, instead of just talking about yourself. Observe someone in your church who is particularly good at asking questions. Curiosity is an intangible skill that we can pray for God to increase in us. This is important because it's hard to get to know someone if we're not curious enough to ask them good questions.*

IDEA #41   *Don't eat alone. Most of us eat three meals a day; that's twenty-one chances to be on mission every week. Meals are an easy way to integrate mission into our lives on a regular basis without adding anything extra to our already busy schedules.*

IDEA #42   *Give cashiers and others in the service industry around town the benefit of the doubt publicly and privately. It'll go a long way towards the non-Christians in your life seeing you as a person of character that they can trust.*

IDEA #43   *Make a list of your friends' birthdays, especially your friends who aren't Christians, and find a way to make them feel awesome on their special day. You may be one of the only people outside of someone's immediate family who takes notice of their special day. This is important because not only do you genuinely care about them, but you also want the gospel to take root in their life.*

IDEA #44   *Regularly write an email of encouragement to a friend who isn't a Christian. Pray that God uses your authentic words of encouragement in whatever way possible so that they will eventually come to see the appeal of the gospel.*

IDEA #45 This is a big one, but start an organization (e.g., farming, medical practice, non-profit, social club, etc.) that will bless your community and create space for mission. Who are some entrepreneurs in the area who are believers and have successfully done this? Make time to get together with them in the next few months to brainstorm and pray together.

Sphere of Influence #4: Your Kids[17]

IDEA #46 Places like McDonald's Playland are often underrated for meeting and interacting with other parents. It's an easy place to start conversations and almost everyone loves talking about their kids. What are some other places in your small town that are underrated for meeting and interacting with other parents?

IDEA #47 Volunteer on a regular basis in your child's classroom. My wife does this on a regular basis in our small town and she's found that, among other things, spending time with kids in a classroom provides a wide-open door to have conversations with their parents at other school events later in the year. Consider praying and asking God how he might want to leverage your involvement in the classroom for the sake of mission.

---

[17] Many of these are ideas are especially applicable if your kids attend public schools.

IDEA #48   *Don't have the expectation that your child's teacher is going to be perfect. Having a posture and attitude of grace towards your child's teacher will go a long way towards them seeing you as a credible and respectable person in town. This will affect the viability of your testimony and mission.*

IDEA #49   *Get creative when giving gifts and notes to encourage your child's teacher. Pray that your sincere encouragement will contribute to tilling up the soil of their heart so that they can eventually hear and respond to the gospel.*

IDEA #50   *If you want to talk to your child's teacher at school, make an appointment instead of just dropping in or asking for a few minutes of their time after school. Teachers are very perceptive; you'd be surprised how knowledgeable they are about which families go to which churches in a small town. This is why simple things like being considerate of a teacher's time go a long ways towards the reputation of the gospel.*

IDEA #51   *Be intentionally complimentary and encourage the people who invest in your kids at school besides their teacher. This might include principals, administrative staff, guidance counselors, aides, and librarians. They don't often get as much attention as teachers but they are an indispensable part of your child's educational experience. Taking the time to appreciate people like this goes a long way towards your testimony to the gospel. In a small town, word travels fast about a person's character—and your character is a vital piece of your testimony.*

IDEA #52   *Teachers often purchase classroom supplies out of their own pockets. Ask your child's teacher about buying extra supplies for their classroom throughout the year. Be as flexible and accommodating as you can because this is an easy way to authentically love your child's teacher and to genuinely display your character. Pray that your deeds would, in some way, point to the reality of the gospel.*

IDEA #53   *Don't skip parent meetings or other activities you're invited to. Lots of non-Christian parents are usually in attendance, so pray that God would open doors for conversations and budding friendships with other parents for the sake of gospel advancement.*

IDEA #54   *If you are a stay-at-home parent, think and pray about how to network with other parents who send their kids to your kids' school. If your kids are in the same classroom, you may have a lot in common. Prayerfully ask God how you can leverage this for mission.*

IDEA #55   *The way you act at your child's school affects the witness of other parents and teachers who are Christians there. This could entail everything from your demeanor and body language at conferences, how much you grumble and yell at your kids' sporting events, or how grumpy you are when dropping your kids off in the morning. In small towns, you'd be surprised how well school district employees and other parents know who goes to which churches. Whether you like it or not, your reputation affects the reputation of other believers at the school.*

IDEA #56   *In many schools, at least one child in your son or daughter's classroom has a rough home life and has parents who are struggling financially to provide for their basic needs. Depending on the particular circumstances, email your child's teacher to see if you can discreetly provide school supplies or other basic needs for a particular student. Pray that your love and care in these kinds of situations will, in some way, bring attention to the grace of God that is found in Christ.*

IDEA #57   *Take full responsibility for your child's bad behavior at school and don't insinuate that the teacher is at fault in any way. Some exceptions exist, but realize that your reputation in a small town will follow you if you choose to shift blame away from yourself and your kids. Little things like this can easily kill mission in a small town.*

IDEA #58   *Be purposeful and become a regular at your neighborhood park so that you and your kids can meet and interact with kids and parents who aren't Christians. It's amazing how many of their peers they'll see at the local park on a Saturday. This is a very strategic way to meet other parents who you'll be interacting with at school or community functions over the next several years.*

IDEA #59   *Go out of your way at your kids' sporting events to talk to parents who might unfortunately and regularly get overlooked. They have stories just like everyone else, and they're probably quite interesting. They might not know any Christians at all and they need the gospel as much as anyone.*

IDEA #60 *Lead the charge in organizing others to help parents of your kids' friends who may have serious needs arise. Not only is this a meaningful way to authentically love people, but it's also an excellent way to display your heart and character for the sake the gospel.*

Q1: What are the five to seven ideas that stand out? Why did they stand out?

Q2: What ideas can you think of in each sphere of influence? Share below.

Q3: What are two to three ideas that God is calling you to implement in your life?

 **WHEN YOU MEET**

- Discuss the three questions in this chapter.

- In what way has your mindset changed after reading this chapter?

- In response to this chapter and your discussion, what is the Holy Spirit leading you to pray about together?

ABOUT THE AUTHOR

Aaron Morrow (M.A., Moody Bible Institute) is one of the pastors of River City Church in Dubuque, Iowa, which was planted in 2016. He and his wife Becky have three daughters named Leah, Maggie, and Gracie.

OTHER GCD RESOURCES

Visit GCDiscipleship.com/books

Jesus does not simply call us to be a lovely community together, but he sends us out to our neighborhoods, towns, and cities to declare and demonstrate the gospel. In fact, the gospel beckons men and women to take up the call of leading and starting communities that are sent like Jesus.

In *Sent Together*, Brad Watson helps leaders discover what it means to start communities centered on the gospel and mission. By exploring the gospel motivations that send leaders to start missional communities, Watson gives readers a framework for the purpose and ways of building a community that is deepening its understanding of the gospel, while also sharing it. *Sent Together* will serve as a field guide for leaders and training guide for those called to start missional communities.

THE STORIES WE LIVE

*Discovering the True and Better
Way of Jesus.*

SEAN POST

Foreword by RICK MCKINLEY

"The Bible as a whole is a story, a grand narrative, that grips our hearts, our minds, our imaginations. We join with Jesus and His community on a quest which demands our best effort in the team's mission. The end is glorious indeed. *The Stories We Live* is a great introduction to that grand narrative and also some of the broken stories which distract many. Read, be gripped by the story, and join the quest!"

Gerry Breshears,
Professor of Theology, Western Seminary, Portland

Make, Mature, Multiply aims to help you become a disciple who truly understands the full joy of following Jesus. With a wide range of chapters from some of today's most battle-tested disciple-makers, this book is designed for any Christian seeking to know more about being a fully-formed disciple of Jesus who makes, matures, and multiplies fully-formed disciples of Jesus.

"*everPresent* does something that most books don't achieve. Most focus either on who God is or what we should do. Jeremy starts with who God is to walk the reader down the path of what God has done, who we are because of God, then points us to understand what we do because of this. I highly recommend picking up *everPresent* to better understand the why and how of the life of those that follow Jesus."

SETH MCBEE
Executive Team Member, GCM Collective

Made in the USA
Middletown, DE
01 January 2017